Everlasting No

Also by Jake Highton

Reporter
Editing
The Spirit That Says No
Nevada Newspaper Days
Against the Mainstream
Saying Nay
No! In Thunder
Disdaining Lies
Disobedience & Rebellion
Facing the Truth
Truths are Treason
Speaking the Truth

Everlasting No

Jake Highton

To Kelley w/ All
Best Wishes,
Jake
5/13/05

On-Call Publishing

Reno, Nevada

On-Call Publishing
Published in 2004
Printed in United States of America
04 03 02 01 00   12 11 10 9 8 7 6

Library of Congress Catalog Card Number: 2003114966
Highton, Jake
        A Collection of Newspaper Columns

ISBN 0-9722487-8-1

The Everlasting No

Carlyle in "Sartor Resartus"

Preface

Thanks once again to the Sparks Tribune of Sparks, Nevada, for publishing my weekly columns that no other Establishment paper would. The columns are constantly critical of U.S. domestic and foreign policy. They are often biting and angry, displeasing many readers of the Trib.

Most of these columns were broadcast as weekly commentary on KUNR, the public radio station in Reno, Nevada. Unfortunately, one column was not broadcast even though I was a regular commentator. Then I was fired by the station.

The censored column was highly critical of John Lilley, president of the University of Nevada, Reno. The news director's gutlessness reminded me of the old newspaper law of Afghanistan. The "law": you were allowed to blast hell out of the Afghans half a globe away and about whom none of your readers cared but locally you had to spike your guns.

The incident also reminded me that censorship, while overt in the former Soviet Union, exists in America although much more subtly. It is self-censorship by publishers and editors, station owners and news editors. This is a little known truth about the media in America with its so-called democracy and mighty First Amendment.

My regular commentary on KUNR was much praised but even more widely condemned. KUNR's news director, to his everlasting credit, deflected irate callers. One caller went so far to say that she loved KUNR but turned off her set when that detestable Jake Highton came on.

But the news director, Brian Bahouth, finally caved in, losing his integrity, violating his conscience and betraying his listeners. He sold out his journalistic soul as nearly every editor, reporter and broadcaster eventually does.

November 2003

Contents

Politics

The Bush nightmare

The American people must realize by now what an abhorrent president Bush is. He violates the social contract and damages the nation. But his photo ops and rhetoric are magnificent.

Take the environment. Plaid shirt. Hiking against the backdrop of forests and mountain scenery. Wonderful pictures for TV and newspapers. Great sound bites. Reality: the Bush "Healthy Forests Initiative" allows increased logging in protected wilderness.

Take Head Start. This federal preschool program has been highly successful for poor kids. Bush would turn this program over to the states, already strapped for money.

More Bush euphemism: his "Clear Skies" plan allows for greater factory pollution. And so it goes. Let's count the ways Bush should be tossed on the ashheap of history:

• Joblessness is at 6.2 percent. Nine million are unemployed. Living below the poverty line: 34.8 million Americans, including 12.2 million children.

• The budget deficit forecast: a record $455 billion this year and half a trillion next year, meaning a huge burden for future generations.

• Bush claimed his tax cut this year would boost the economy and create jobs. False. Progressive magazine rightly calls the cuts "one of the most brazen redistributions of income to the wealthy that this nation has ever seen."

• Everyone sees Bush chatting up the nine rescued Pennsylvania coal miners. Almost no one knows that he cut black lung benefits and funding for mine safety.

• Bush poses as a corporate reformer. Everyone sees him sign a bill to curb the criminality of Enrons. Almost no one knows that he guts the enforcement budget for the Securities and Exchange Commission.

• Bush promises to leave no child behind. His tax cuts eliminated tax credits for families of 12 million poor kids.

• Everyone sees Bush praise U.S. troops, triumphantly wearing a flight suit to land on a carrier. Few know that his administration wanted to reduce overseas and combat pay.

• Bush loudly proclaims his devotion to national service but forces AmeriCorps to suffer devastating cuts for its volunteer program.

• Bush praises federal civil servants for their "hard work and unwavering dedication" but curtails their pay increases.

• The Bush administration consistently manipulates scientific data to serve its ideology and corporate donors, shattering the integrity of bodies that monitor food and medicine, conduct health research, control disease and protect the environment.

• More manipulation: information on condoms is removed from government Web sites.

• The Bush administration cooks the intelligence books just as Enron *et al* did.

• Bush is privatization mad: much of the military, much of the sacred national parks and Social Security.

• Bush violates the separation of church and state that presidents have held dear since the founding of the nation.

• Bush pushes long-range development of hydrogen-powered cars while adamantly opposing increased fuel efficiency for today's autos.

• His highly touted "comprehensive energy plan" is the same old same old: subsidies and tax breaks for oil, gas and coal industries. It does not address U.S. dependence on foreign oil. It does not address global warming.

• The appalling secrecy of the Bush administration. It censored 28 pages of a 9/11 report. It extends suppression of presidential papers.

Then there is the huge, huge matter of credibility. Bush waged war in Iraq with lies and deceptions. Now Iraq is looking more and more like Vietnam. As Ruth Rosen, San Francisco Chronicle columnist, writes:

"Like ghosts from the past, words and phrases from the Vietnam era—quagmire, credibility gap, guerrilla war, winning the hearts and minds of civilians, the call for more troops—are creeping back into military and public parlance."

America is bogged down in Iraq and Afganistan. No light is at the end of the tunnel. Deaths of U.S. soldiers in the Iraqi occupation outnumber combat deaths. The occupation costs $4 billion a month—not counting vast reconstruction costs. As New York Times columnist Bob Herbert puts it: "the war we so foolishly started in Iraq is a fiasco—tragic, deeply dehumanizing and ultimately unwinnable."

Moreover, every "reason" for the war was fraudulent. Saddam Hussein was not linked to al Qaeda, he had no nuclear or other weapons of mass destruction, Iraq was no threat to America and there was nothing to the Pinocchio-nose report of Iraq getting uranium from Africa.

Bush belies at every turn the very Christianity he professes to espouse. Reason enough to end the nightmare.

Sparks Tribune, Sept. 4, 2003

The American booboisie

"Plus ça change, plus c'est la même chose" came to mind while reading Zola's novel, "La Débâcle," while observing typical American reaction to the U.S. invasion of Iraq.

A character reflects at the start of the Franco-Prussian War in 1870 about crowds sweeping down the boulevards of Paris, brandishing torches and crying: "To Berlin! To Berlin!" Then he adds: "He could still hear the voice of a tall, handsome woman with a majestic profile…wrapped in the folds of a tricolor and singing 'The Marseillaise.' "

So it was with *boobus Americanus*.

Actors Tim Robbins and Susan Sarandon, stars of the baseball film, "Bull Durham," were rightly critical of the U.S. war in Iraq. For that offense against superpatriotism, the baseball Hall of Fame president canceled the 15th anniversary showing of the film at Cooperstown, N.Y. The president, an imbecile named Petroskey, said their criticism could put U.S. troops in danger.

Some Canadians who wintered in Arizona were told not to come back to their trailer park next year. Why? Canada opposed the war. Canadian trucks returned from the United States with graffiti urging truckers to STAY IN CANADA. Canadians visiting the United States have been verbally abused.

Boobery turns into cretinism.

Then there is the French-bashing because the French had the wisdom to oppose the war even though most nations also refused to join "the coalition of the willing." The willing included such mighty nations as the Solomon Islands. French officials visiting Washington are buffeted with "resentment and anger."

A deputy war secretary says Turkey made a huge mistake by not letting U.S. forces use its country. The Bush adminstration continues to treat the United Nations with disdain, giving it a tiny role in Iraqi reconstruction.

During a long buildup to the inevitable war, President Bush came out almost daily with a new rationale. Some were:
- Iraq had weapons of mass destruction.
- Saddam Hussein posed a threat to America.
- Iraq supported international terrorism.
- Iraq had nuclear ambitions.
- Iraq had chemical and biological weapons.

Every "reason" a lie.

Such falsehoods were akin to covering up the United Nations replica of Picasso's great antiwar painting, "Guernica," to avoid the glaring irony of a pro-war speech by Secretary of State Colin Powell.

The Bush triumphalism turned demagogic with his Top Gun landing on a Navy carrier so close to the San Diego skyline that the ship had to be turned around to show the sea. Here was the often AWOL Texas air guardsman—who pulled wires to avoid Vietnam—posing in a flight suit. The staged event, costing taxpayers $1 million, will be shown *ad nauseam* on TV during the 2004 presidential campaign for gullible Americans to lap up. Then Bush had the gall to proclaim triumph over Iraq "one victory in a war on terror."

Then there is the unspeakable crudity of war secretary Donald Rumsfield. He said war and freedom are untidy, "stuff happens" and compared Hussein with Hitler.

Then there was the outrageous flag-bedecked cars boasting of beating up a fifth rate army exhausted from wars against Iran and America, devastated by 12 years of sanctions, without an air force and suffering from overflights and blockades. The mayor of New York urged a ticker tape parade on Broadway for the veterans of a war that could have been won with U.S. air power, its sophisticated technology and the New York City police force.

In short, it was not really a war but a slaughter, a TV

7

entertainment. It was like pitting the worst high school football team against Notre Dame. And it exemplied the Bush doctrines of preventive war, global dominance, tattered international relations, damnation of world opinion and fearmongering over 9/11. The invasion of Iraq was one more example of U.S. imperialism that began 105 years ago with the seizure of the Philippines, Cuba and Puerto Rico.

It was, in the words of columnist Robert Scheer, "an egregious abuse of power that rises to the status of an impeachable offense."

U.S. barbarism—recalling the Mongols sacking Baghdad in the 13th century—was symbolized by the looting of the Baghdad museum of antiquities. U.S. troops stood by while priceless objects from the Cradle of Civilization were carted off. This despite the fact that scholars had been warning the Bush administration for months about its treasures. However, America *did secure* oil fields.

What is desperately needed is a regime change in Washington.

Sparks Tribune, May 15, 2003

'INVADE IRAQ'!

When Teddy Roosevelt became president in 1901 on the assassination of William McKinley, the Republican boss of New York, Tom Platt, muttered that now that "damn cowboy" is in the White House.

Today we have another damn cowboy in the White House, George Bush II: warmonger, imperialist and unilateralist. He is a menace to the world.

Bush is determined to invade Iraq. No rational argument, no doomsday scenario, will deter him. He is like the Supreme Court under Chief Justice Rehnquist: if you want an outcome, you manufacture reasons to do it. Or, as the French say: *se faire une raison* (to make oneself a reason).

Bush and his reprehensbile minions, Cheney and Rumsfield, come up with a new argument for an invasion every day: Hussein has weapons of mass destruction...a regime change is essential...he is evil personified...he harbors and abets terrorists with biological and chemical weapons...he has a horrible history of striking without warning..."an urgent duty to prevent the worst from occurring."

Yet the reasons against a U.S. war in Iraq are compelling. America has absolutely no business policing and bullying the world. The moral and ethical arguments against war are plain:

Passage by Congress of a resolution to use force is not a declaration of war as required by the Constitution. War violates international law, mocks the U.N. charter, fails the "just war" test and fails the *casus belli* test.

Indeed, the United Nations was founded to prevent wars of aggression such as the one Bush intends to launch. Allies? Europeans are quesy. Only Britain's Tony Blair, Bush's butler, is with the warhawks.

U.S. hypocrisy is beyond belief. America has thousands of nuclear weapons, Iraq doesn't have one. China has 20 nuclear weapons. Logically, why not invade China? America has chemical and biological weapons just as Iraq does. In fact, the Bush I administration provided Iraq with the means to wage chemical and biological war.

Why not attack the U.S. client state of Saudi Arabia? Fifteen of the 9/11 hijackers were Saudis. Iraqis is not linked to al Qaeda. Freedom? America only mouths freedom. Saudi Arabia is an autocracy.

The Bush policies of pre-emptive strikes and anticipatory self-defense are breathtaking in their hubris. And the consequences of war are vast. Deaths on both sides could be high, the destruction great. The cost will be enormous. It will further inflame the Arab world, already angry at the United States for condoning the brutish Israeli policy in Palestine.

An ad in the New York Times by the journal *TomPaine.common sense* put the case perfectly. It pictures Osama bin Laden with his finger pointing at the reader with the headline: "I WANT YOU TO INVADE IRAQ." The copy says:

"Go ahead. Send me a new generation of recruits. Your bombs will fuel the hatred of America and their desire for revenge. Americans won't be safe anywhere. Please, attack Iraq. Distract yourself from fighting al Qaeda. Divide the international community. Destablize the region. Make my day."

Why war? Oil and politics.

Iraq controls 10 percent of the oil in the Middle East. America wants to control that oil as it already controls Saudi Arabian oil.

War would be a marvelous diversion from Bush's political problems. It would make voters forget that the economy is failing badly, forget the widespread corporate criminality leading to loss of pensions and jobs, and forget the deficits that will grow with warp speed once war starts.

Yes, Bush goes through the motions of seeking

approval of Congress, the U.N. General Assembly and Security Council. But that's just pretense. Bush intends to make war even if God himself were to counsel against it.

The problem for the anti-war movement is that leading Democrats, wanting to face the electorate next month as war-supporting "patriots," sit supinely while Bush and his hawks want to "let slip the dogs of war." As Marc Cooper of the LA Weekly asks:

"When it becomes so patently obvious that the administration's warmongering stems not at all from any authentic security concerns but rather from cold and cynical domestic political calculation, why is there no clear...anti-war opposition?"

Hussein is not a clear and present danger to the United States or its neighbors. The United States has no right to invade sovereign nations and overthrow their leaders. It is monumental arrogance to think it does.

Far from being unpatriotic to oppose a second Iraqi war, it is a consummate act of patriotism to resist it. Bush's warmongering pours oil on a world already inflamed.

Sparks Tribune, Oct. 17, 2002

U.S. rogue nation

The clamor for war with Iraq for the past six months has masked the truly appalling foreign policy of the Bush administration.

From repudiation of the International Criminal Court to reducing grants to the U.N. Population Fund, that policy is as abhorrent as the Bush domestic policy.

The administration has abandoned any pretense about a family of nations. It stands above international law. It is bellicose and unilateralist. It ignores U.N. resolutions. It refuses to sign the human rights convention.

The United States goes it alone in its pursuit of the right-wing agenda. And it can do it with impunity because it is the only superpower on the globe.

Lloyd Axworthy, former Canadian foreign minister, notes correctly: "Any illusion that the U.S. administration might have a smidgen of respect for international treaties or multilateral co-operation should be finally dispelled. Americans will resort to crude means to wreck any form of international architecture with which they disagree."

America opposes treaties to eliminate greenhouse gases, prohibit land mines and ban testing of biological weapons. It defies a U.N. plan to enforce a convention on torture.

It and Somolia are the only nations refusing to sign the Convention on the Rights of Children, claiming that they undermine parental authority, condemn capital punishment and lead to abortion. America drastically scales back funding to fight worldwide AIDS, the No. 1 killer in history.

The Bush II Doctrine declares that the United States can launch pre-emptive attacks on any "evil" nation that possesses nuclear, biological or chemical weapons. Hence, oil-rich Iraq is the target of an imminent war—although many countries without oil are not targeted.

James Galbraith, writing in the American Prospect, warns against this empire-building: "To maintain (an empire) against opposition requires war—steady, unrelenting, unending war. And war is ruinous—from a legal, moral and economic point of view."

And Galbraith might have added: huge casualties among military and civilians of "enemy" nations in U.S. wars that are little more than shooting fish in a barrel.

Bush sweeps contrary opinions under the rug. When the Environmental Protection Agency submitted a report contradicting what the administration has claimed about global warning, Bush dismissed it as a mere product of "the bureaucracy."

Democracy? Mouth honor, as Shakespeare calls it. But no word about ally Egypt condemning a man to seven years of hard labor for advocating democracy. Free trade? Sure. But America slaps a higher tariff on imported steel. It slaps a higher tariff on Canadian lumber. Politics triumphs over principles.

Bush skipped the U.N. Earth Summit, refusing to address global environmental threats and "flipping off" Third World concerns about the shocking gap between rich and poor nations.

Another U.S. refusal: an international treaty that would ban cigarette advertising and sports sponsorship as part of the World Health Organization's drive to curb smoking. WHO notes that 4 million people worldwide die annually from smoking-related diseases.

But the United States opposes a ban, arguing that it would violate the First Amendment guarantee of free speech. Nonsense. The First Amendment is a great bulwark of American liberties. But peddling a killer product is a legitimate reason for government to bar it from advertising. Commercial speech can be curbed. Non-commercial speech cannot.

More American insistence on "my way or the

highway." It engineered the ouster of Mary Robinson as U.N. commissoner of human rights. It pulled the plug on Robert Watson, head of the panel on climate change. Their fault: not doing the bidding of the United States.

In the Middle East, Bush has "promised" a Palestinian homeland in three years but does nothing to end Israel's illegal military occupation while building settlements.

Nor does the admistration have an answer for Edward Said's *cri de coeur*: the Israeli government plans "nothing less than the obliteration of an entire people by slow, systematic methods of suffocation, outright murder and the stifling of everyday life."

U.S. troops are stationed all over the globe, from Afghanistan to Uzbekistan. U.S. soldiers are in the Philippines, Indonesia, Somalia, Yemen and the Sudan. America is the global cop.

Meanwhile, a former German foreign secretary, has Bush dead to rights. He calls Bush "the most intellectually backward American president of his political lifetime, surrounded by advisers whose bellicosity is exceeded only by their political, military and diplomatic illiteracy."

The United States is the *real* rogue nation.

Sparks Tribune, Dec. 5, 2002

U.S. gores U.N.

The French have been better Americans than we have.
Jonathan Schell, The Nation

Nothing better illustrates *boobus Americanus* than the widespread animosity, anger and outrage at the French for daring to oppose the barbarian U.S. invasion of Iraq.

The antediluvian Dennis Hastert, speaker of the House, proposed putting an orange danger label on bottles of French wine. Some absurd Americans have dumped French wine. Others have called for a boycott of French cheeses like brie, Camembert and Roquefort. This ridiculousness extends to calling french fries freedom fries.

The French are called intransigent. They are called ungrateful for the U.S. intervention in world wars I and II. But the French are absolutely right, America absolutely wrong.

The U.S. invasion is unjust, unlawful, morally indefensible and without world sanction. It is pre-emptive. And it is unilateral except for Bush's poodle, Tony Blair of Great Britain. But such U.S. barbarities are all too frequent as the most casual reading of history will show.

Far more serious than French-stomping childishness is the U.S. assault on the United Nations. The U.N., by charter definition, exists to provide worldwide peace and human rights.

But to Bush, the U.N is irrelevant. It's his way or the highway despite the fact that Iraq is no threat to the United States, no threat to the world and unlinked to terrorists. Like a boy king, Bush stamped his feet and sent the troops into Iraq. All along he wanted U.N. and Security Council approval as a fig leaf for his imperialism. His administration sought to bully the U.N. as it bullies—or bribes—other nations.

It is not U.N. failure. It is U.S. failure. America once

again has not lived up to the high ideals of freedom and democracy that it is constantly preaching. The Bush motto: world collaboration be damned.

The U.N. charter says:

• "All members shall settle their international disputes by peaceful means. (Ignored by Bush.)

• "All members shall refrain in their international relations from the threat or use of force against the territorial integrity or political independence of any state." (Violated by Bush.)

• "The only grounds for a country acting alone is "if an armed attack occurs against" it. (Ignored by Bush.)

As Matthew Rothschild, editor of Progressive, writes: "Bush returns international relations to the raw power politics of the 19th century and abandons international law for the law of the jungle."

But then the hubris of the United States to attack any nation whenever it wishes is an old, old story. America warred in Vietnam, Cambodia and Laos without approval of the U.N. Security Council. It attacked Panama, Grenada, Dominican Republic, Libya, Somalia and Sudan without U.N. sanction.

America is also terribly selective about what U.N. resolutions it wants enforced. Yes, Iraq has violated 17 Security Council resolutions. But Israel is the world's No. 1 violator: 32 of them. Unfortunately, Israel is a U.S. client and hence untouchable. But Iraq, once courted by the United States, is now labeled evil.

The United States has become the No. 1 wielder of violence by unleashing its bombs and missiles, its napalm, bunker busters and fragmentation bombs. And what is heavy U.S. bombing of Baghdad if not terrorism? America has engineered coups and destablized nations. It tries to assassinate heads of any regime that stands in the way of its efforts to make the world safe for inhumane capitalism.

An exchange of emails by two Renoites, who love their country but love justice even more, is instructive. One writes: "We operate under the staggeringly arrogant assumption that American and good are somehow synonymous." The other writes: "We have set a horribly dangerous precedent in attacking a non-belligerent country that did not attack us, our allies or its neighbors. We have brazenly assumed a new posture of supreme arrogance and recklessness in the world."

The Iraq invasion masks terrible domestic truths: the budget is in freefall, joblessness is rising, the economy is staggering and states are in financial crisis so they cut funding for essential educational spending and social services.

As the Progressive put it in an editorial: "So enthralled is Bush with the might of the Pentagon, so enraptured is he with his self-assigned role of liberator, so sure is he of doing God's will, that he has become an enormously frightening figure. He seems to believe he can rule the world alone."

The Bush war means Mars triumphs over justice and humanity. It means America has lost its moral compass, its very soul.

Sparks Tribune, April 10, 2003

Bush: soulless un-Christian

Not being a theologian, perhaps I should not venture into the treacherous waters of a man's theology. Nevertheless, it seems to me that President Bush's professed belief in Christianity is belied by his every action.

The message of Christ is nothing if it is not concern for the poor, for making society more just and humane. Indeed, there is more communism in Christ than Christians will admit. (Jesus angrily overturning the tables of moneychangers in the temple.)

Bush is anything but the compassionate conservative he pretended to be when campaigning for president. He is anything but Christlike with his programs and pronouncements.

Examples abound. He will unleash "the dogs of war" on Iraq, lusting for battle in a most un-Christian way. (Matthew 16:26: "For what is a man profited if he shall gain the whole world but lose his own soul?")

He insists on tax cuts for the wealthy in a most un-Christian behavior. (I Timothy 6:10: "For the love of money is the root of all evil.")

A real Christian would be concerned about the Have Nots, the Have Littles and Have Not Muchs. He would be concerned that 40 million Americans don't have health insurance. He would be angered that the minimum wage of $5.15 is pitifully low. He would not make welfare mothers work 40 hours a week instead of 30 even as he shrinks childcare funds by $61 million.

Head Start is a highly successful federal program serving one million poor preschool children. It enables kids—not privileged as Bush was—to get a fairer start in kindergarten. Bush would turn this program over to the untender mercies of the states. States, already strapped for money, are cutting back on so many essential services. Bush would cut $13 million in programs to aid abused and neglected kids. (Mark 10:14: "Suffer the little children to come unto me and forbid them not for such is the kingdom of God.")

Surely it is not Christian for Bush to devastate the sacred environment so business can make ever more money. (Matthew 4:4: "Man shall not live by bread alone.")

But it is in taxing policies that Bush is most un-Christian. He insists on cutting taxes by nearly $700 billion over 10 years. Who would benefit most? The rich. The top 1 percent of Americans. Those making $374,000 or more would save $34,000 each. (Matthew 6:24: "Ye cannot serve God and mammon.")

Meanwhile, 20 percent of low-income earners will get a tax cut of $6.

Columnist Molly Ivins sums it up so well: "One-third of all Americans will never see a dime of that tax cut. Half of all taxpayers will get less than $100...Those who make more than $1 million a year will get an average cut of $92,000." (Matthew 19:24: "It is easier for a camel to go through the eye of a needle than for a rich man to enter the kingdom of God.")

Among the beneficiaries would be rich people like Bush and Vice President Dick Cheney. Bush would net a mere $44,500 compared with Cheney's windfall of $327,000. Is anything more obscene, more un-Christian than that?

Bush is like those 13th century editorial writers at the Wall Street Journal who call people making $12,000 a year "lucky duckies." Why? Because they receive government services but pay *only* 4 percent in taxes.

Payroll and sales taxes mean such people are actually paying 20 percent of their income in taxes. Ivins notes: "Most of us actually pay more in payroll taxes than we do in income taxes." As she adds, Federal Insurance Contributions Act taxes stop at $87,000— benefitting the rich.

Most Americans stoutly insist that this is a classless society. But nothing could be farther from the truth. Bush is a past master of class warfare. He wants to abolish inheritance taxes, paid only by owners of the wealthiest estates. He wants to abolish the stock dividend tax, paid mostly by the rich.

What is that if not class warfare?

It certainly is class warfare when the United States has the most unequal distribution of wealth in the Western World. It certainly is class warfare when 1 percent of Americans own 40 percent of the wealth.

You could go so far as to argue that you cannot be a Christian *and* a Republican. In any case, what good are all those biblical injunctions that Bush keeps hearing at church if he ignores them? Bush is not just un-Christian. He has no soul—either in the theological or secular senses.

Sparks Tribune, March 20, 2003

Bush the reactionary

George W. Bush is the most reactionary president the nation has ever had.

The roll of 43 U.S. presidents is studded with mediocrities and non-entities such as John Tyler, Millard Fillmore, Franklin Pierce and James Garfield. But none has ever been as retrograde as Bush II.

Only a political naif believed the Bush PR slogan during the 2000 campaign that he was a compassionate conservative. In office, this *soi-disant* compassionate conservative:

• Sics his attorney general on people who need to smoke marijuana to alleviate intense pain and other medical ills.

• Sics his attorney general on Oregon's humane death-with-dignity law.

• Hampers stem cell researchers—who could cure such diseases as Alzheimer's—by severely restricting their funds.

• Insists on tax cuts for the rich and repeal of the estate tax that only plutocrats pay.

• Cuts money for job training and child care for women trying to get off welfare while insisting that they work 40 hours a week instead of 30.

• Withholds contribution of $34 million to the U.N. population fund. Why? His fear of abortion is far greater than his concern for thousands of deaths and enormous human misery.

• Refuses to push a women's bill of rights treaty that 170 countries have ratified.

• Cuts Superfund moneys to clean up toxic waste at 33 sites in 18 states.

• Oks ever more snowmobiles in Yellowstone and Grand Teton national parks.

• Eases clean air rules to allow polluting power plants to get bigger without having to get cleaner.

Meanwhile, the rebarbative Bush cabinet includes: the

war-hungry secretary of defense, Donald Rumsfield; the civil liberties-destroying attorney general, John Ashcroft; the anti-environmentalist secretary of the interior, Gale Norton; and secretary of health and human services, Tommy Thompson, who wants to redefine a fetus as a child eligible for federal funds despite a Supreme Court ruling to the contrary.

The Tartuffish Bush calls for freedom for Cubans but cracks down on U.S. citizens who want the freedom to travel to Cuba. He pretends to be upset by corporate piracy while spurning legislation that would prevent U.S. firms from relocating to tax havens offshore.

He poses happily for a photo-op with rescued coal miners from Pennsylvania while cutting funds for mine safety. Bush pats black kids on the head in other sickening photo ops while doing nothing about the inner cities. He devastates the environment but a photo op on page one of the New York Times shows him hiking the Adirondacks on Earth Day.

The Bush judicial nominees are from the political dark ages. They are of the stripe of his favorites justices, Antonin Scalia and Clarence Thomas. (Bob Herbert, New York Times columnist, rightly calls Thomas "a gruesome acolyte of Scalia who has spent much of his time on the Supreme Court taking a pickax to black interests.")

Bush tried to foist the racist Charles Pickering on the 5th U.S. Circuit Court of Appeals. Two dozen Pickering rulings as district judge were reversed by the 5th Circuit, the most conservative of the appeals courts.

Bush named Brooks Smith, who calls the Violence Against Women Act unconstitutional, to the 3rd U.S. Circuit Court of Appeals. He named Michael McConnell, who has violently opposed Roe v. Wade, to the 10th U.S. Circuit Court of Appeals.

Bush named Miguel Estrada to the U.S. Court of Appeals for the District of Columbia Circuit. Estrada has a name appealing to Latinos, making Senate opposition politically difficult. But Estrada is awfully conservative.

Other reactionary Bush policies:

• His foolish and totally unrealistic abstinence-only sex education program for teenagers.

• His administration's campaign of disinformation and intimidation that hobbles nationwide AIDS prevention.

• His call to industry for *volunteer* steps to reduce injuries from repetitive motions on the job.

• His call for workers to rely on lawsuits, which have taken up to 10 years to litigate, to resolve ergonomics woes.

• His approval for the timber industry to log millions of acres on national forest land "to prevent catastrophic fires."

• His relaxation of air quality standards governing coal-fired power plants to the detriment of the health of nearby residents.

The gap between the Bush imagery and reality is gaping. No other U.S. president has so ruthlessly torn the nation's social, economic and environmental fabric.

Sparks Tribune, Nov. 21, 2002

Be Democrats, damn it

The cure for the Democratic Party sickness is simple: Democrats must act like Democrats rather than as clones of Republicans.

Democrats must realize that it is far better to lose by advocating the right principles than to lose by offering the wrong principles. As the Brits say, you might as well be hung for stealing a sheep as a lamb.

Yet some Democrats say that the party must be *still* more moderate. Hooey. If it becomes any more moderate it will be the right wing of the Republican Party.

For two decades it has heeded the backward Democratic Leadership Council. That way is failure. If Democrats are ever to regain power they must attack reactionary Republican policies.

Here's what the Democrats must do in the runup to the 2004 presidential election:

• Denounce a permanent tax cut that will mostly benefit the wealthy. Denounce the administration's plan to repeal the estate tax for the benefit of a few superrich.

• Urge a universal health care system.

• Urge universal child care payments.

• Make the right to join a labor union a civil right, a right so necessary in these union-busting times.

• Seek a national law prohibiting striker replacement.

• Denounce GOP plans to privatize Social Security.

• Attack the blatant GOP effort to deny blacks the vote. Evidence: hiring black youths holding signs saying not to vote for Democrats, telling people they can't vote unless they pay back rent and intimidating black voters in order to suppress Democratic turnout.

• Demand public financing of all elections.

• Urge free college education for all who meet

admissions requirements, a program like the enormously successful GI bill after World War II.

• Push a plan for energy independence that will cut the link to oil.

• Call for an increase in the paltry minimum wage.

• Attack the Bush administration for allowing snowmobiles in sacred national parks like Yellowstone and Grand Teton.

• Fight for clean air and water against an administration that favors the polluters. Clamor against global warming. Oppose more logging in national forests. Oppose drilling for oil in pristine parts of Alaska.

• Point out how taxpayers are forced to pay for cleaning up after polluters.

• Denounce rampant corporate crime. Denounce corporate tax evaders setting up overseas havens.

• Blast the way the GOP has stacked the regulatory agencies with people who eviscerate controls.

The Democratic Party desperately needs these messages. It must be confrontational. Me-toism won't draw people to the polls.

Voters must be made to realize that, in the words of Frank Rich, New York Times essayist, the Bush administration tailors "every conceivable policy, including those governing human, fiscal and environmental health, to the needs of its corporate sponsors."

Admittedly, it is tough to beat an imperial president who conceals important issues by hawking war and prating about security. But it is these other issues that will win the hearts—and votes—of millions of Americans.

Moreover, Democrats must jettison the leaders that have led only to disaster. That means Senate Democratic leader Tom Daschle who meekly surrenders to Bush. It means discredited and feckless people like Terry McAuliffe,

Democratic Party chairman. It means so-called Democrats like the reprehensible Joe Lieberman.

Democrats desperately need new messengers.

Maybe it has found one in Rep. Nancy Pelosi, the new Democratic leader in the House. She scores 100 percent in ratings by Americans for Democratic Action, organized labor and environmental, consumer and human rights groups.

Oh, she is being derided as a "latte liberal," sneered at as a "San Francisco Democrat" (Republican code words for being a lover of gays and lesbians). But the truth is that it would be a far, far better country if it were just half as liberal as San Francisco.

Most Americans are not rich. They are ordinary folks who would be grateful if Democrats stood for them.

The GOP, on the other hand, speaks for the special interests. It pursues class warfare on behalf of the rich. It pushes the right-wing religious agenda. It does not speak for the vast majority of Americans.

Sparks Tribune, Jan. 23, 2003

Racism pays off for GOP

The Trent Lott outrage reveals to the public what has been apparent for four decades: the Republican Party's not-so-subtle appeal to segregation and the Confederacy.

The once Solid South for the Democrats has become the Solid South for the GOP because of a yearning for the "good old days" of racism, reaction and repression. Days of Black Codes, lynchings and whites-only lunch counters, bathrooms and drinking fountains.

Oh, none of this is put so baldly by the Republicans. They use code words. But the facts are incontrovertible. The GOP has cosied up to racists.

It wins election after election in the South with racial appeals, by subtly displaying its white sheets. It appeals to white racist men while trying relentlessly, desperately and unconscionably to keep blacks from voting.

Sen. Theodore Bilbo, archconservative Mississippian who intimidated blacks to keep them from the polls, died in 1947. But his white supremacy and demogoguery is still very much alive in the Republican Party.

It started with Richard Nixon and his Southern Strategy. Then we had Ronald Reagan. Then we had Bush I followed by Bush II. Only the names change on the presidential ballot in the GOP's relentless racial pitch.

Nixon's ugly Southern Strategy involved an appeal to racist voters. Reagan campaigned in the South in 1980 as an advocate of states' rights, a code word for segregation.

As Joseph Crespino, history professor at George Mason University, put it: "the Reagan campaign made an unmistakable effort to identify with the people, language and symbols of the South's segregationist past."

Bush I ran the outrageously racist Willie Horton ad to win the White House in 1988. Bush II ran a smear campaign in South Carolina in 2000 against Sen. John McCain with a barrage of emails, phone calls and leaflets claiming that McCain had a black child (actually an adopted daughter from Bangladesh).

During the campaign, Bush II spoke at Bob Jones University, a citadel of virulent anti-Catholicism whose brand of ultraconservative Christianity did not tolerate interracial dating. The signal was clear: Bush was on their side.

Bush campaigned for Georgia's governor-elect in 2002, a candidate whose main issue was restoring the Confederate flag.

The Bush II judicial nominations have been chosen to please the Right and to signal support for Southern racist views.

Jesse Helms of North Carolina was twice elected to the U.S. Senate by flashing a blatant race card.

Nor is Lott alone in his love for the Confederacy. Attorney General John Ashcroft has called Confederate leaders patriots. He has lauded Missouri's pro-Confederate government in exile.

Ashcroft extolled Southern Partisan magazine, which celebrates the assassination of Lincoln, defends slavery and praises Nathan Bedford Forrest, the founder of the Ku Klux Klan.

One of the most sickening photos of all time appeared in the New York Times recently. It showed smiling, laughing and clapping blacks at a rally for the racist Lott at the Mississippi capitol.

Didn't these Uncle Toms knew that Lott has voted consistently against civil rights legislation, opposed an extension of the Voting Rights Act, decried the creation of a Martin Luther King holiday and voted against the first black judge on the 4th U.S. Circuit Court of Appeals because he was black?

That Lott favored measures to outlaw busing for school segregation? That he sought to eliminate affirmative action in federal contracts? That he has consistently opposed affirmative action?

That he has consorted with the segregationist White Citizens' Council? That he told the neo-segregationist Council of Conservative Citizens that it had "the right principles and the right philosophy"? That he has tried to roll back the gains of the New Deal and the Great Society?

That he is proud of racist Dixiecrat Strom Thurmond? That he wished Thurmond had won in 1948? That Thurmond stood for segregation forever?

Lott is no aberration.

Republicans, with more subtly than Lott, have capitalized on what columnist Robert Scheer calls the "real, powerful, cancerous" racism that still haunts the nation. Their party's disgraceful behavior has hurt blacks, the nation and progressive politics.

Yet at the end of the Lott affair we heard that he should resign for the good of the Republican Party—not for the good of black people.

The fact is that while party leaders finally disavowed Lott, forcing his resignation as Senate majority leader, President Bush continued to play to his Southern constituency by renaming to the federal courts racists and segregationists.

For 40 years Republicans have abandoned the party of Lincoln. Bob Herbert, New York Times columnist, is right: the GOP has become "a safe house for bigotry."

Sparks Tribune, Jan. 9, 2003

Guardian of the Left

Sen. Paul Wellstone of Minnesota had integrity where integrity is so rare: in politics.

He was one of the precious few Democrats who dared invoke the glories of the Roosevelt New Deal, one of the precious few politicians who proudly called himself a liberal, one of the precious few politicians who guarded the Left.

Wellstone, who died recently in a plane crash, was the conscience of Congress. He was especially important in these days of wimpish Democrats.

A measure of the man was the vote he cast against the Iraq war resolution. Nearly all the gutless members of Congress who faced a stern re-election challenge voted for the resolution.

Another measure of the man was indicated by his bid for the Senate in 1990. He campaigned in a rundown green school bus, wore a work shirt and stayed in people's homes rather than hotels. Even more astonishing in this day and age: he wrote his own speeches.

Wellstone ran on a shoestring budget. In a memorable ad, the audio and video were speeded up with Wellstone saying he had to talk fast because he didn't have $6 million to spend as his opponent did.

He was fiercely independent, a maverick in the tradition of Oregon's Sen. Wayne Morse. He opposed the big bucks corrupting politics and the adventurism of the Bush administration.

He spoke for the poor and dispossessed, a constituency with almost no votes. He championed the little guy, the rights of workingmen and women, the family farmers. He battled for unions. His targets were banks, agri-business and corporations. He fought for the environment.

Paul Krugman, economics columnist for the New York Times, wrote: "The most consistent theme in his record was economic, his courageous support for the interests of ordinary Americans against the growing power of our emerging plutocracy."

Wellstone's intense feeling for the underdog came from his working- class parents. He had no money to go to college. But he was a good high school wrestler so he won a scholarship to the University of North Carolina. Having earned a doctorate with his thesis on the roots of black militancy, he taught political science at Carleton College in Minnesota.

Another measure of the man: when Carleton custodians went on strike, he held classes off campus rather than cross a picket line. Wellstone fought the college's investment in companies doing business in then apartheid-oppressed South Africa. He walked the picket line with strikers at a meat-packing plant. He railed against repeal of the estate tax, rightly arguing that most of the benefit would be for the rich.

No wonder Dennis Myers, Trib columnist, said: "He was the kind of politician who, by his good example, made other politicians embarrassing to watch."

One of the finest tributes came from an unexpected source: conservative Sen. Phil Gramm of Texas: "A man of conviction, who never swayed from his beliefs even when fighting a lonely battle."

Bill Holm, Minnesota poet and essayist, wrote: "Paul charmed—and sometimes persuaded—even those hostile to his unashamed liberal ideas by listening with great courtesy and attention to unfriendly questions.

"He answered without dissembling, without backing down from his own principles but with a civil regard for the dignity of the questioner...He voted as he spoke—from the heart."

In Minnesota years ago at a journalism conference, an out-of-state professor was chatting with a professor about

Wellstone. "My God," the Minnesotan exclaimed, "he's to the left of Gorbachev." (Mikhail Gorbachev was then head of the Soviet Union.)

The remark was meant to be pejorative. But actually it was a great compliment, a compliment all too seldom paid in the sickeningly conservative politics of the United States.

Maureen Dowd of the New York Times wrote that Wellstone was immediately beatified after his death. She had a point. The fact is that Wellstone did vote *for* wars in Afghanistan and Yugoslavia, did vote *for* the Defense of Marriage Act, did vote *for* the USA Patriot Act and did vote *for* sanctions against Iraq.

But no politician is ever perfect. Wellstone was justly praised for his integrity and courage, a man widely admired even by political opponents.

Wellstone told voters what he thought, not what they wanted to hear. It is so rare for politicans to vote their convictions rather than what they know will boost their re-election chances.

These days nearly everyone runs for office claiming to be the people's candidate. Such pols are phonies. Wellstone was for real.

Sparks Tribune, Nov. 7, 2002

Eurodisaster: demise of Left

The Left, moribund for decades, died in the recent French elections.

France, one of the most civilized countries in the world, has a great tradition of revolution and man-the-barricades radicalism. Yet it has succumbed to a European malady. It has consigned socialism to the scrap heap of history.

The European march to the right has been inexorable. From Austria to Portugal, a conservative curtain has fallen across Europe. It is an unmitigated Eurodisaster.

For years now we have had Tony Blair, British prime minister, run pell-mell to the right. He more and more resembles Margaret Thatcher, former right-wing prime minister who denounced labor as "the enemy within."

Blair's Labor Party, which once championed the poor and working class, now talks of cracking down on crime and launching military strikes against Iraq. It lets for-profit firms run public services like trains and buses—and some schools and prisons too. Meanwhile, public health and transportation services deteriorate.

In France, Socialist Premier Lionel Jospin offered nothing more than conservative platitudes in the presidential primary. He pushed privatization and pro-market policies. His government was for fiscal austerity, free trade and lower taxes. He flirted with the conservative cry: law and order.

Jospin, for God's sake, even admitted that he was a socialist but that his "platform was not socialist." No wonder Jospin lost to a genuine conservative, President Jacques Chirac on the Gaullist right.

As further proof of the Left's demise, Robert Hue, leader of the once-strong French Communist Party, lost his suburban Paris seat.

In Germany, the only major center-left party, the Social Democrats headed by Premier Gerhard Schröder, is trailing in the polls to a conservative challenger in the September elections.

Center-left governments and coalitions have lost office in Belgium, Denmark, Italy, the Netherlands, Norway and Portugal. The shibboleths of the Right are crime, immigration and political corruption. The Right also yammers about the quickening pace of the European Union, causing what right-wingers perceive as a loss of national identity.

In France, with a history of anti-Semitism going back at least as far as the Dreyfus case, anti-semitism is rearing its ugly head again with firebombing of a synagogue in Marseille and the desecration of Jewish cemeteries.

Even Holland, the freest country in the world, has seen the rise of the Right. In recent Dutch elections, far-right parties have joined government coalitions. Soon we could see right-wing governments forming a majority among the 15 nations of the European Union.

In Norway and Switzerland, although both countries are not in the EU, xenophobic parties are muscling their way into mainstream politics. In Austria and Switzerland, anti-immigrant parties won 27 percent of a recent vote.

Here in America, the Right is not only transcendent, it is in power and wielding that power ruthlessly. His Fraudulence was given the White House by just five out of 300 million Americans. Then he ushered in the Reactionary Age that makes President Reagan look like the moderate he never was.

President Bush has repealed everything good that President Clinton promulgated: ergonomics regulations to protect workers, road-building in national forests and a ban on snowmobiles in national parks. He has gutted the Clean Air Act. Bush finds global warming and pollution just great.

His attorney general, John Ashcroft, is dangerous: assaulting civil liberties, the rights of man and common decency.

Rep. Tom DeLay, House majority whip, says he is on a mission from God to promote a "biblical worldview." That worldview, if you read the Old Testament, consists of mass murder, genocide, destruction and rape. (See 1 Samuel 15:3 where the "Lord of hosts" urges Israelites to "smite Amalek and utterly destroy all that they have...slay both man and woman, infant and suckling, ox and sheep, camel and ass."

True, there are tides in the affairs of mankind. The pendulum swings from left to right, from revolution to counterrevolution, from reformation to counterreformation and vice versa.

But the conservatives are in the saddle now. Socialism, the best hope for governing mankind, is being rejected nearly everywhere.

Sparks Tribune, Aug. 8, 2002

Blame GOP deregulation

Deregulation, deregulation, deregulation. And more deregulation. That's the problem in California, not Gov. Gray Davis.

As columnist Robert Scheer notes: the underlying woe for all states is a national economy crippled "by the fall of a panoply of corrupt companies, firms such as Enron, which used the Republican mantra of deregulation as a cover for looting consumers, stockholders and employees...California has paid a particularly heavy price for the machinations of Enron and other energy companies."

That loot: billions of dollars. The robbery in California netted the Enron bandits $45 billion. The heist was pulled off by market manipulation of Enron and other energy companies, spiking energy prices and creating artificial shortages.

Columnist Paul Krugman of the New York Times writes that California was "the victim of one of the worst abuses of market power since the robber baron era."

Montana is facing the same evil. Its residents used to pay some of the lowest power rates in the Northwest. Now, under deregulation, they pay among the highest rates in the Northwest.

Columnist Molly Ivins writes that former California Gov. Pete Wilson caused the mess that Davis inherited. Wilson made utility deregulation "the centerpiece of his administration," arguing that it would mean lower prices and "a new age of better, cheaper, more reliable energy."

But the magic hand of Adam Smith worked for just the corporate few.

Nor is the Bush White House blameless in this whole shabby affair. The Bush-dominated Federal Energy Regulatory Commission "failed to bring the energy pirates to heel," Scheer notes. Moreover: the recall "conveniently distracts from the alarming failures and frauds of the White House," including the "administration's blind eye to the energy sting that robbed California."

Why the Bush nonchalance? "Kenny Boy" Lay, former Enron CEO and once close friend of President Bush, has been a major contributor to the Bush family political campaigns.

Yes, California has a large budget deficit. (Not $38 billion, columnist Krugman says. He calls the projected gap for next year $8 billion.)

Yes, Davis is as bland as his first name. He has been too conservative, pro-Big Business and all for law and order. (Although, scared by the recall effort, he is reinventing himself as a liberal.) Nevertheless, to recall him is absurd, a gross abuse of recall elections.

The U.S. Constitution calls for impeachment of a president for "treason, bribery or other high crimes and misdemeanors." Davis has done nothing to merit "impeachment."

The fiasco was engineered by Republicans angered over the fact that the California GOP consistently loses races for the U.S. Senate and governorship. The coup attempt was organized by ultraconservative Republicans and bankrolled by Rep. Darrell Issa of California with a contribution of $2 million.

Moreover, if Davis is recalled, a candidate can be elected to replace him with something like 15 percent of the vote. The ballot lists 135 candidates—with no runoff—meaning the vote will be badly divided. Hence, a pitiful plurality wins.

Still another villain in California's fiscal woes is Proposition 13. The measure, passed in 1978, lowered by 60 percent and strictly limited property tax increases. That led to the state's reliance on the volatile income tax while local governments were starved for funds.

Prop 13 is madly regressive, the wealthy paying far fewer taxes on property than they should. This leads to such gross disparities as the case of investor Warren Buffett, economic adviser to Arnold Schwarzenegger. Buffett pays $14,401 in property taxes on a $500,000 home in Omaha, Neb., but just $2,264 on a $4 million home in California.

That is being overtaxed only in the warped mind of Schwarzenegger, who is running on his movie celebrity with platitudes, evasions and refusal to debate—and artful dodging of questions. Californians enamoured of him might find the lesson of Gov. Jesse Ventura of Minnesota instructive. A pro wrestler, Ventura is leaving Minnesotans a legacy of huge deficits and drastic slashes in essential public services.

Moreover, Ruth Rosen, columnist for the San Francisco Chronicle, notes that Davis signed landmark legislation: "the nation's most progressive legislation on women's reproductive rights, a statute giving farmworkers more power in labor negotiations with growers and the country's first bill to ban toxic flammable chemicals that threaten public health."

Smart Californians will vote no on the recall Oct. 7 while casting a second ballot for Lt. Gov. Cruz Bustamante in the event that Davis loses.

Sparks Tribune, Sept. 25, 2003

Democracy at its worst

Democracy is that system of government under which the people, having 35,717, 342 native born adults to choose from, including...many who are wise, pick out a Coolidge to be the head of state. It is as if a hungry man, set before a banquet prepared by master cooks...should turn his back on the feast and stay his stomach by catching and eating flies.

H.L. Mencken definition of democracy

Yes, yes. It's pitifully anti-democratic and snootily elitist to say so. But democracy is rule by ignoramuses.

Example: the recent folly in California where Gov. Gray Davis was recalled and Arnold Schwarzenegger elected to replace him.

This is not a plea for restoration of monarchy. Monarchy is detestable as the French had the wisdom to see in the 18th century and the Brits still cannot see in the 21st century. But it is to say that too many people are stupid about voting.

The recall election was democracy at its worst, provoking contempt for the herd and its Mass Mind.

By electing a movie star as governor, Californians proved once again that they know nothing about governing and everything about Hollywood. They preferred the simplistic phrases of a celebrity while accepting his ignorance on issues and refusal to discuss them.

Why, for God's sake, would 31 percent of Latinos vote for Schwarzenegger when a Latino, Lt. Gov. Cruz Bustamante, was on the ballot? Why, for God's sake, should 42 percent of women vote for the misogynist, sexist, groper and boorish Schwarzenegger?

Such lack of political judgment means democracy is rule by the unenlightened. Such ill wisdom is proved time and time again. California has a terrible habit of electing people like actor Ronald Reagan as governor and a song-and-dance man George Murphy as U.S. senator.

Nationally, most of the 43 presidents have been mediocrities and non-entities. The few good presidents, like Franklin Roosevelt, are accidental. FDR was elected because of the Depression. Just about any Democrat could have defeated Hoover in 1932.

I.F. Stone, one of the all-time greats of U.S. journalism, rightly answered the sloganeering of the 1960s about power to the people: "If you give power to the people, we'd all be in jail."

Witness the "three strikes and you're out" law passed by California voters, a measure worthy of the 18th century. It means a man committing three felonies—even if the third is stealing three golf clubs—is sentenced to 25 years in jail. It means sentencing a man to 50 years in prison for stealing a couple of kid videos. It means voters showing their inhumanity.

When the law was challenged in the U.S. Supreme Court as cruel and unusual punishment outlawed by the Eighth Amendment, Justice Sandra Day O'Connor provided the fifth vote to uphold it. She said any criticism of the law should be directed at the legislature not the courts.

Her argument is specious. Lawmakers, reflecting the will of the people, will not repeal it. They do not want to be perceived as soft on crime. Moreover, if she was a real judge instead of an ideologue, she would have seen the law for what it is: unconstitutional.

Witness the tyranny of the majority in Maine five years ago. Maine voters made theirs the first state to repeal its law protecting homosexuals from discrimination. They nullified a law barring discrimination against gays in housing, jobs, public accommodations and obtaining credit.

The recall and initiative were measures espoused in the Progressive Era to give the people "in the street" more say in the political process. Fine. But California pushed the initiative to absurd lengths. It has voted in a plethora of laws, including the infamous Proposition 13 of 1978 that robbed schools of property tax revenues.

Ever since that ill-advised measure it has become almost impossible to raise taxes anywhere. In Nevada, any revenue increase requires a two-thirds vote in each house. This is tyranny of a superminority.

As Ted Rall notes in his Web column: "Isn't it time to admit that direct democracy doesn't work?" Yes. Proposition 13 and the farce of the recall prove it.

Mencken wrote this devastating truth: "Democracy is a form of worship. It is the worship of jackals by jackasses." No wonder he constantly railed against *boobus Americanus.* No wonder he wrote: "No one...has ever lost money by underestimating the intelligence of the great masses of plain people."

Sparks Tribune, Oct. 16, 2003

Social Issues

Big Brother looms

The Orwellian nightmare is upon us. The Patriot and Homeland acts are civil liberties disasters as the nation moves inexorably toward a police state. Americans are now at greater risk of intrusion from their own government as Big Brother becomes all too real.

Under the Homeland Act, government agents can scan email, tap telephones, monitor credit card purchases, and check bank transactions and travel patterns while shielding themselves from scrutiny by exemption from Freedom of Information requests.

Creation of the Homeland Security Department by Congress is a bureaucratic nightmare, combining 22 agencies in a cabinet-level organization. But far worse is what the populist newsletter, the Hightower Lowdown, calls a seismic change. Specifically, it :

• "Authorizes the most massive concentration of police power since World War II."

• "Reverses dozens of crucial Supreme Court rulings on the Bill of Rights."

• "Allows the government, which these days is more in partnership with giant corporations than the American people, to spy on every resident of the country—and for the first time to take the Internet into its orbit of control."

Secret arrests are now permitted. The criteria for those secret arrests are—you guessed it—top secret. The standards for colored-coded terrorism levels are secret.

Aside from those civil liberties horrors, the acts contribute little to national security and do nothing about intelligence-sharing between the CIA and FBI.

The Senate Judiciary Committee issued a report recently noting that the FBI has done a poor job fighting terrorism, wraps its efforts in excessive secrecy and analyses information poorly.

The truth is inescapable: the FBI spends far too much time, effort and money battling trivia.

Attorney General John Ashcroft had 10 FBI agents spend 13 months investigating a brothel in New Orleans. It nabbed 12 prostitutes—a great triumph for Western Civilization.

The FBI chases dead-beat fathers, puts a key terrorism investigator on a piddling arson case and spends inordinate time fighting the bogus drug war. This is a terrible waste of talent. But that's nothing new.

In the name of national security, the FBI spent two decades conducting unlawful operations at the University of California in Berkeley. It schemed with the head of the CIA and a member of the California Board of Regents to harass students, faculty and regents.

It campaigned to destroy the career of UC President Clark Kerr, sending to the White House derogatory allegations about Kerr that the bureau knew were false. It falsely portraying him as pro-communist. It targeted 54 professors who subscribed to "subversive publications." It snooped on "illicit love affairs, homosexuality, sexual perversion and excessive drinking."

The Hoover-era snooping still goes on. The FBI keeps files on "subversives"—anyone who dares criticize government policies. More waste of time, talent and money.

Nor is police statism really new. The FBI counterintelligence program, under the despicable J. Edgar Hoover, infiltrated, monitored and disrupted anti-war, civil rights, church and black organizations. Martin Luther King, surveilled and persecuted by the FBI, was denounced as a "communist tool," Adlai Stevenson as a "notorious homosexual."

As David Cole, Georgetown law professor, says: "When investigations go on and on for years and focus entirely on lawful political activity, the FBI is not only wasting its time but violating constitutional rights." (Not that the CIA or FBI ever cared about the Constitution.)

The FBI abuse of power is appalling. The enemy is terrorism—not political dissent.

Loch Johnson, public affairs professor at the University of Georgia, has noted: "Democracy and spying don't mix very well. Secrecy runs counter to democratic accountability. Openness threatens the success of espionage. We need the CIA and FBI to acquire information that may protect us but we recoil at having secret agencies in our open society."

Finally, the Homeland Security Act makes a corrupt bargain with corporations. It allows the department to contract with firms that set up dummy fronts in the Caribbean to avoid taxes. Patriotism be damned.

Speaking of patriotism. Under the Patriot Act librarians must reveal to investigators books taken out by subscribers. Agents can enter homes without notice and detain U.S. citizens without charge or access to a lawyer.

The New York Times puts it perfectly: "These accounts of the FBI's malfeasance are a powerful reminder of how easily intelligence organizations deployed to protect freedom can become its worst enemy." And ours.

Sparks Tribune, March 27, 2003

Corporate crime damns capitalism

The fault, dear Brutus, is not in our stars but in capitalism. The "invisible hand" of capitalist preacher Adam Smith, who said that individual gain benefited the whole society, has always been a lie.

No further proof need be cited than the corporate scandals that have ravaged America this year. Thousands of people have suffered from this grand larceny.

President Bush can rationalize the corporate corruption as a "few bad actors." Fed reserve chairman Alan Greenspan can speak of infectious greed. But neither faces the truth: capitalism works only for the few, not the many.

The bill of indictment is vast: obscene CEO salaries and stock options, insider loans and fraudulent bookkeeping to jack up stock value and overseas moves to avoid taxes, labor costs and environmental regulations. (WorldCom overstated pretax profits by an incredible $3.8 billion last year.)

The bursting bubble of capitalism in the outrages of Enron, WorldCom, Global Crossing *et al* caused the loss of millions of dollars in personal savings, pensions and stockholdings and left thousands jobless.

Progressive magazine explains the why of the corporate chicanery: "Corporate executives have a tremendous incentive to cut health care coverage, renege on pensions, bust unions, pick up stakes and move to any country that offers the lowest wages and the least regulation."

That incentive: impress Wall Street with ever-higher stock prices. This madness for profits means the public be damned. Morality and capitalism are contradictions in terms.

Jack Welch, former CEO of General Electric, was paid insanely and given enormous perks. Salary and bonus in 2000: $16.7 million. Perks: household expenses for a palatial apartment, including food, wine, staff, laundry, dry cleaning and utilities.

More perks: Boeing 727 business jet, helicopter, limousines, rental cars and security personnel. And still more perks at sports events: courtside seats, skyboxes and elite golf courses.

The evil of capitalism has been vastly increased by Congresses hellbent on deregulation ever since the lamented Reagan era. Those corrupt Congresses, in repealing New Deal controls on corporations, were in bed with the crooks they should have been regulating.

And the reason is clear. Corporations supply the money for politicians' campaigns. It is legalized bribery. No campaign-funding reform will rein in the bastards until elections for national office are publically funded.

Because of congressional giveaways, we have WorldCom, once a fiber optics behemoth, reporting net income of $3.5 billion between 1996 and 1998 yet receiving a tax rebate of $113 million. The notorious stock options sheared $265 million off its tax bill.

Meanwhile, we have Paul O'Neill, treasury secretary of the reprehensible Bush administration, saying that the nation creates "economic prosperity, not by strangling people with… regulation…but by opening up the world." We have Vice President Cheney saying that corporate America should not be drained of its risk-taking spirit and harm the economy.

Tell that to distraught former corporate employees.

President Bush has shown stunning hypocrisy about all this. He pretends he is Franklin Roosevelt attacking "economic royalists." He has the chutzpah of the Jewish boy who killed his parents then threw himself on the mercy of the court because he was an orphan.

Bush was on the board of Harken Energy Corp., which gave him *loans* to buy stock that he then parlayed into a lucrative investment with a Texas baseball team. He got *four* Harken stock transactions that netted more than $1 million. Each time he was suspiciously months late in reporting the sales to the Securities and Exchange Commission.

How different Bush is from another Republican president, Teddy Roosevelt. TR, who was more Left than Democrats are today, let alone Republicans, urged as a Progressive Party candidate in 1912 that the nation adopt heavily progressive taxes on corporations and individuals.

To him, this was social justice, redistributing wealth so that all citizens would have a decent life. This was *real* patriotism, not the phony flag-flying sort. But Roosevelt's plea was ignored in this far too conservative country. The whole political system is rigged for the few at the top.

Most Americans should be enraged into voting Democratic in November. As Matt Rothschild, editor of Progressive magazine, put it in quoting his father: "The Republicans care about only two things: God and greed—and in no particular order."

Sparks Tribune, Sept. 22, 2002

Neanderthals assault unions

Union-busting has been rampant in America for decades but absolutely nothing will be done about it. Here's why: all the commanding heights in this class warfare are held by labor's enemies.

President Bush would like to eliminate unions. Congress, with Republicans controlling both houses, is hostile to labor. The Supreme Court is controlled by ideologues who will manufacture reasons to oppose unions—and damn the Constitution. The National Labor Relations Board is so stacked with Republicans that it might as well be called the National Management Relations Board.

The House of Labor is helpless against such might. But that is nothing new. Throughout most of history the American labor movement has been beset by enemies: laws, courts, cops and armies, and legislatures and executives in federal and state governments. You don't have to be a bleeding heart to become angry when reading that shameful history.

The Wagner Act of 1935 is nearly a dead letter. It gives workers the right to organize and bargain collectively. But all across the land people are being fired for attempting to organize unions. Workers are intimidated. They are told that if they unionize the company will move elsewhere.

Anne-Marie Cusac gives grim statistics in Progressive magazine: "25 percent of companies fire one or more workers for union activity during union campaigns, 75 percent hire anti-union consultants, 92 percent force employees to attend captive-audience meetings, and 52 percent threaten to call the immigration service if the union drive involves undocumented workers.

"The power of government to police such brazenness is limited and many employers believe the benefits of breaking the labor laws far outweigh the risks. As a result, millions of workers remain unrepresented and at the mercy of employers."

Nonunion workers are most at the mercy of bosses. The federal minimum wage of $5.15 is laughably low. Companies like Wal-Mart get obscenely wealthy by busting unions.

Striking unionists are often permanently replaced. Companies trot out hordes of lawyers. Even if workers win in the lower courts, appeals drag the cases out for years.

Bush made Eugene Scalia solicitor general of the Labor Department. Scalia? He called ergonomics quackery—junk science—despite the fact that 1.8 million Americans are injured each year by bad ergonomics.

A three-part series in the New York Times recently noted that workplace rules are too weak and too weakly enforced. Even if firms violate those rules they are fined absurdly low amounts. About 200,000 workers have died from on-the-job injuries since 1972. Yet the Bush budget slashes funds for the Occupational Safety and Health Administration.

The Bush transportation team has declared that collective bargaining for federal airport screeners is inappropriate. In the new Homeland Security Department, 170,000 federal workers can be fired at will by the president.

General Electric, the nation's most profitable company, will force workers to pay more for their health coverage. Never mind that the company nets $16 billion in annual profits. Never mind that Jack Welch, former CEO, gets $17 million annually and perks worth another million.

And for those naïve enough to believe the Supreme Court is nonpartisan, the court's decision last year in Hoffman v. NLRB is instructive. The dominant Reactionary Five ruled that a chemical plant worker was not entitled to $67,000 in back pay even though he was illegally fired for union organizing. The court said the law meant nothing because the worker was in the country illegally.

Dissenting Justice Breyer clearly saw the truth: the ruling allows firms to hire illegal immigrants then freely fire them—"with a wink and a nod"—if they try to start a union.

Immigrants, who take jobs that most people don't want, lack benefits, lack child care and lack a living wage.

In these terrible days under Bush, the House of Labor is near collapse. Union rolls have declined precipitously in the past four decades. Just 13.5 percent of workers have union representation today as opposed to 39 percent at its peak in 1954.

The Patriot Act promises to privatize 850,000 government jobs. The Homeland Security office declares that union membership is harmful to the common good. And Bush doesn't even bother to return phone calls by John Sweeney, president of the 13 million-member AFL-CIO.

Yet it will get still worse for unionism with reaction in all the saddles.

Sparks Tribune, April 17, 2003

Wal-Mart the 'terrorist'

Wal-Mart is the world's largest retailer, the world's largest private employer and the world's largest corporation. It is also the world's most visciously anti-union company. It is not illegal to unionize at Wal-Mart—it's just next to impossible to do so.

Wal-Mart has turned union-busting into an art form: powerful videos, copious propaganda pamphlets, compulsory meetings to preach anti-unionism, excess hirings to dilute union voting strength, surveillance of pro-union workers, sudden pay raises to induce anti-union voting—and firings, always firings for pro-union workers.

When the butchers' department of a store in Texas did vote to unionize, Wal-Mart abolished *all* butcher departments.

It's a form of terrorism that exemplifies the exploitation and the cruelness of capitalism.

Wal-Mart's anti-union fervor enables it to undercut prices elsewhere and make $7 billion annual profit. It pays pitifully, offers niggardly benefits, batters work rules and forces employees to work off the books (no overtime pay as required by law).

Here in Nevada, the Wal-Mart behemoth is so frightful that a bill has been introduced in the Assembly requiring grocery chains to offer health insurance or pay the state for health care it may have to provide.

Unionized Kroger workers make $14 to $17 an hour after three years. At Albertson's it is $15.63 plus full health and pension benefits. The comparable scale at Wal-Mart is $10 to $12. Some Wal-Mart workers qualify for welfare. Others get food stamps or have the state pay medical expenses because they can't afford health insurance.

Medical insurance is so costly at Wal-Mart that just two in five employees buy it.

Barbara Ehrenreich, researching for her book, "Nickel

and Dimed," worked for $7 an hour at a Wal-Mart in Minneapolis to see if she could make expenses while paying her rent. She could not.

Wal-Mart has about 3,300 stores and 1.2 million employees. Corporate headquarters in Bentonville, Ark., commands stores in nine countries. The nation's largest retailer, it has three branches: retail stores, Sam's clubs (even greater discounts for members) and supercenters, combining retail and grocery stores.

The wage slaves are called associates. But few workers fall for that euphemism. The annual turnover is 70 percent company-wide, meaning about 700,000 people quit each year. But Wal-Mart's doesn't care. One of its operating philosophies is to hire a replacement at $7 an hour rather than pay $10.50. Another of its dirty tricks is stopping employees from working more than 32 hours a week so they are ineligible for medical coverage.

Sexism is rampant in the company. Earlier this year a class action suit was filed against Wal-Mart, alleging gross discrimination against women employees. One study showed women making $1,100 less than men in comparable jobs. Women store managers make $16,000 less than men. Highly qualified women are passed over for promotion.

Wal-Mart likes to argue that men "have families to support." Well, so do women, particularly single mothers.

The National Organization for Women labels Wal-Mart a Merchant of Shame. Columnist Jim Hightower is even stronger: "It's famous low prices are the product of human misery."

Another problem for women has been Wal-Mart's refusal to post openings for management positions. This allowed women to be bypassed in favor of the Old Boy Network .

Another serious problem with unions at Wal-Mart is the toothlessness of the law. Labor law is much like what Dickens described in "Bleak House." It grinds so slowly.

Cases drag on and on. Wal-Mart, with money to burn, appeals even when it has no valid grounds.

A U.S. administrative judge ruled last fall that three Wal-Marts in Las Vegas broke the law repeatedly by confiscating pro-union literature, denying promotion to employees because of their union support and interrogating workers about pro-union leanings.

Then there is a matter of overseas sweatshops. Wal-Mart has several thousand toy factories in China. Workers are paid 13 cents an hour.

Columnist Hightower notes that the Chinese workers live in company dorms with 12 to a small room while working 13- to 16-hour days, seven days a week and 20-hour shifts. "They literally are sick of work thanks to the 'paint dust' that constantly hangs in the air as well toxic glues, thinners, plastics and other solvents," he writes.

It's easy for progressives to plead: boycott Wal-Mart. But, unfortunately, they will never convince people. It's human nature to love bargains. Moreover, some people on the financial thin edge *need* the big cost savings of Wal-Mart.

Sparks Tribune, May 8, 2003

Affirmative action for privileged

President Bush relishes photo ops with black people, jamming them into pictures with him at White House announcements and on every visit to public schools. See, he loves blacks.

But photo ops are PR. The reality is otherwise. Bush reached the apogee of political hypocrisy on Martin Luther King Day recently when he announced his opposition to affirmative action.

This from a man who used affirmative action to get into Yale. He was unqualified but got in through a legacy appointment. (His father went to Yale.) Earlier he used affirmative action to get into Phillips Academy in Andover, Mass. (He was unqualified but his father was an alumnus.)

Mike Luckovich, editorial cartoonist of the Atlanta Journal and Constitution, wryly captured the Bush gambit. He has Bush saying after the King Day announcement: "I have a dream that one day men will not be judged by the color of their skin but by their alumni connections."

Aside from stunning hypocrisy, Bush lies about affirmative action to make his case. He denounced what he called quota systems in the University of Michigan case now before the Supreme Court.

It's the Big Lie technique of the propagandist: reverse discrimination, racial preference—hot button words for unfairness.

But Michigan does not use quotas. It gives extra points to applicants who belong to an underrepresented racial or ethnic group. It also gives points to applicants who come from the white Upper Peninsula, scholarship athletes and men in nursing studies.

Michigan, like most elite colleges, uses race as just one of many diversity factors. And diversity is absolutely necessary. It enables colleges to admit students from different geographical areas and different cultural and social backgrounds.

Academia, of all places, must be hospitable to different perspectives, different voices and different experiences.

Most of us live in a white world: housing, job, worship, social. Affirmative action helps open up colleges to essential racial integration for the benefit of us all.

Bush says affirmative action is "unfair and impossible to square with the Constitution," that it is un-American. Oh? A Constitution that condoned slavery? A Constitution that counted blacks as three-fifths of a man? A Constitution that condoned Jim Crow for more than 100 years?

Affirmative action is essential. It helps rectify a legacy of state-supported racism, a legacy of poverty, humiliation, dehumanization and degradation.

Wealthy whites, in contrast, have a huge advantage socially, politically and educationally. Yet Bush would deny affirmative action to blacks. As Maureen Dowd, New York Times columnist, asks: "Isn't it un-American if the University of Michigan—or Yale—makes special room for the descendants of alumni but not the descendants of the disadvantaged?"

Is it un-American to use affirmative action for black Americans who for centuries were denied educational opportunity? No.

And what about legacy? Just two generations ago blacks were denied admission to the universities of Texas and Virginia. Princeton—once racist Princeton—did not admit blacks until World War II.

Even after World War II, in which black troops fought with honor, black veterans could not stay in white hotels or eat in white restaurants. They were denied equal educational opportunities and denied the right to vote.

Blacks start with a huge disadvantage. Julian Bond, NAACP chairman who has called black gains of the past four decades the second Reconstruction, rightly says that affirmative action is "the most effective tool for advancing entry into the mainstream."

"A black child is one and one-half times more likely to grow up in a family whose head did not finish high school than is a white child," Bond points out. "Two times as likely to be born to a teenage mother..three times more likely to live in a single parent home...and four and a half times more likely to live with neither parent."

As UC Berkeley history prof Leon Litwack puts it: "For almost our entire history, affirmative action has been a prerogative of white males." But affirmative action has been under constant assault because it threatens that white-skin privilege.

W.E.B. DuBois, great black scholar and activist, said the problem of the 20th century would be the problem of the color line. Opposition to affirmative action shows that it is still a problem in the 21st century.

Sparks Tribune, Feb. 13, 2003

Covenants with death

Most major nations reject the barbaric death penalty. But the United States, still hundreds of years away from becoming civilized, persists in this barbarity.

America clings to the long discredited biblical notion of an eye for an eye and a tooth for a tooth. Families cling to the long discredited notion of retribution, for what they call closure. And lawmakers, not wanting to be targeted as soft on crime, cling to the barbarous practice.

So when Gov. George Ryan of Illinois emptied Death Row of 167 convicts before leaving office, the pundits complained, right-wing talk shows screeched and Ryan's friends shunned him. But Ryan, noting that the death penalty kills innocent people, rightly questioned the fairness of the whole process.

"Our capital system is haunted by the demon of error, error in determining guilt and error in determining who among the guilty deserve to die," Ryan said.

He was right. But commutations are not enough. Abolition is the only answer. Capital punishment is un-Christlike. As Camus put it in his fine essay, "Reflections on the Guillotine," capital punishment is an "outrage to the person of Christ."

In the judical-murder scheme false confessions have often been coerced or falsely reported by police. Eyewitnesses are often mistaken. Jailhouse testimony is often outright lying. Prosecutors often put pressure on defendants. Court-appointed lawyers often give the most perfunctory counsel. One Chicago "cop shop" is infamous for using torture to wring confessions.

By continuing this judicial killing, the United States imitates autocratic nations like China and Iran. (Iran recently hanged a youth for drinking alcohol.)

Twelve states have abolished the death penalty.

Unfortunately, Nevada is not among them. But Ryan's action, the most sweeping cleansing of Death Row in history, should cause some legislatures at least to reopen the capital-punishment debate.

"The Education of George Ryan," as the New York Times headlined an editorial, is instructive. As a conservative Republican in 1977, Ryan voted in the Illinois legislature to reinstate the death penalty. But he grew in office, grew as a human being—grew as we all should.

Over the years Ryan has had nagging doubts about capital punishment: false accusations of murder, DNA revelations and the arbitrariness of the whole process. So, first he ordered a moratorim on executions. Then he took a huge step by converting death sentences to life sentences.

Ryan noted that people in rural Illinois were five times as likely to be sentenced to death than someone convicted of murder in Chicago. He also pointed out that the Death Row population in Illinois was overwhelmingly black and that 35 had been condemned by all-white juries. (A recent study found that defendants in Maryland were more likely to be sentenced to death if they are black and accused of killing someone white.)

The Supreme Court, after correctly calling the death penalty unconstitutional in 1972, wrongly reinstated it. Lately it has at least been taking small steps to correct some of the gross abuses in the grisly business of capital punishment.

The court ruled last year that executing the mentally retarded was cruel and unusual punishment barred by the Eighth Amendment. It then held unconstitutional state statutes that permit judges to impose the death sentence after conviction by juries.

Unfortunately, the likelihood of the Rehnquist Court abolishing capital punishment is nil. Reactionaries like Chief Justice Rehnquist and his partners in crime, Justices Scalia and Thomas, lust to see people killed by the judicial system.

The court desperately needs a majority of justices like William Brennan, Thurgood Marshall and Harry Blackmun to call the death penalty what it is: cruel and unusual punishment. As Brennan wrote in a 1972 opinion: "The calculated killing of a human being by the state involves…a denial of the executed person's humanity…uniquely degrading to human dignity."

And then we have John Ashcroft, the hanging U.S. attorney general. He frequently overrules federal prosecutors who recommend against the death penalty. Naturally it rankles them. But it satisfies Ashcroft's blood lust.

The European Union is right to insist that no country can become a member if it has not abolished capital punishment. While Defense Secretary Donald Rumsfield can sneer at "old Europe," Europe has its priorities right. It knows that capital punishment is abhorrent.

Sparks Tribune, Feb. 20, 2003

Environmental daily outrage

We've been able to gut one environmental protection regulation after another...we've speeded up logging in national forests, rolled back protections of 58 million acres from roads and developments, eased pollution controls for power plants, rejected new fuel-efficency standards...removed limits on coal producers for dumping mountaintop fill in streams, reduced EPA fines of polluters, halted funding for several superfund sites, replaced scientists who don't support our views, rejected the Koyoto global warming treaty and much more.

Doonesbury comic strip
with a voice from the White House

Every word is true. Nothing is funny about it. The assault on the environment by the Bush administration is tragic. It has rolled back more than 200 laws and regulations that protect public health and the environment.

Things are so horrible with Bush in the White House that Nation magazine has a column on its Website called "The Daily Outrage." (www.thenation.com)

The latest environmental outrage by the Bush administration is an effort to get exemptions for pesticides scheduled to be phased out by 2005 under a treaty to eliminate ozone-depleting chemicals.

No matter that the treaty, the Montreal Protocol of 1987, was ratified by 160 nations including the United States. No matter that the protocol is one of the most effective environmental accords. No matter that the pact was designed to end the use of the chemical compounds that damage the ozone layer protecting Earth from ultraviolet radiation. To the Bushites, money-making and business are all that matter.

President Bush in his State of the Union address called for a half-billion dollar reduction in the budget for the

Environmental Protection Agency. He proposed trimming $100 billion from the Agriculture Department's hugely successful wetlands preservation program.

His Clear Skies Initiative sounds great but does nothing about carbon dioxide pollution that contributes to global warming. In fact, his proposal would allow more pollution than is permitted by law. Another great White House euphemism is the Healthy Forest Initiative. Reality: it gives carte blanche to the timber industry to ravish national forests.

The White House pushes dirty air, polluted rivers, fouled streams, disappearing wetlands and drilling in national parks. But so what? The opinion of the vast majority of the American people counts for nothing in this arbitrary, arrogant and atrocious administration.

The Interior Department received 360,000 comments via email or letter on snowmobiles in Yellowstone and Grand Teton national parks. Eighty percent of the writers wanted to ban the machines. The department did the opposite, adopting the Vanderbilt cry that the public be damned.

Arianna Huffington noted in Sierra magazine some of the regulations trashed by the Bushites: rules miminizing raw sewage discharges, a regulation prohibiting the government from awarding contracts to firms that violate environmental laws, requirements that mining companies protect waterways and pollution, rules banning personal watercraft in eight national parks, and Army Corps of Engineers regs barring the dumping of industrial waste in rivers and streams.

As Mark Hertsgaard wrote recently in The Nation: "No administration since the dawn of the modern environmental era 40 years ago has done more to facilitate degradation of the ecosystems that make life on Earth possible."

The only good environmental news from the Bush

administration: it backed off its ignominious proposal to raise the level of arsenic in drinking water.

The Bushites also:

• Will replace up to 70 percent of full-time National Park Service jobs with private-sector employees and volunteers as part of its plan to privatize 850,000 federal workers. In other words: replace professionals with amateurs.

• Will permit widespread logging in the Giant Sequoia National Monument in California. In other words, as President Reagan infamously said: "If you've seen one redwood you've seen them all."

• Will abandon the principle that the polluter pays, shifting the cost of cleaning up toxic Superfund sites from the polluters to the taxpayers.

Bush has extolled President Teddy Roosevelt. But he ignores the wisdom of TR who said: "The nation behaves well if it treats the natural resources as assets which it must turn over to the next generation increased, and not impaired, in value."

In short, Bush has absolutely no understanding or feeling for what Aldo Leopold, the late, great environmentalist, called the land ethic. "The land ethic," he wrote, "simply enlarges the boundaries of the community to include soils, waters, plants and animals or, collectively, the land."

Sparks Tribune, March 6, 2003

Bush assault on abortion

President Bush is so determined to overthow Roe v. Wade, Supreme Court decision liberating women from unwanted childbearing, that the recent 30th anniversary of the decision was no cause for celebration.

While Bush awaits the chance to pack the Supreme Court with anti-abortion justices, he has taken repressive measures to smother a civil right of women.

His administration has denied $34 million appropriated by Congress for the United Nations population fund because it allegedly condones abortion. Result worldwide: 2 million unplanned pregnancies, 800,000 induced abortions and about 4,700 maternal deaths and 77,000 infant deaths.

Bush's cruel policy has devastated people's lives. About 120 million women who either wanted to space children or stop having them are unable to get contraceptives.

The Bush administration has reinstated a gag rule for recipients of U.S. family planning funds aboard. At home, it backs the Child Custody Protection Act prohibiting anyone but a parent from taking a teenage girl across state lines for an abortion. (Crossing a state line to an abortion clinic may be much closer and much cheaper.)

Bush tripled funding for the head-in-the-sand abstinence sex education program. He named as attorney general John Ashcroft, a violently anti-choicer. He names staunchly anti-abortion judges to the federal courts.

A U.S. delegation to the recent population conference in Bangkok tried to block an endorsement of condoms to prevent AIDS. Fortunately, it failed. The conference rejected the U.S. position thunderingly, 32-1 and 31-1.

The New York Times noted the routine embarrassing behavior by the Bush administration at international meetings on women and health: "Most Americans would be shocked at the lengths their representatives are going to in their international war against women's right to control their bodies."

Ditto for domestic policies.

A fetus is now considered a person. The Bushites promulgated a federal rule allowing states to redefine fetuses as unborn children, making the mother eligible for benefits in health programs for low-income families.

The states have hardly needed encouragement, already undercutting Roe severely. Twenty-one states require mandatory waiting periods. Forty-three states have parental notification laws, 28 limit financing and 28 have passed laws that aim to put abortion clinics out of business.

If Roe is overturned, the nation would return to dangerous back-alley and coat-hanger abortions. During the 1960s, 1 million American women had illegal abortions. About 5,000 died from botched operations.

The right to abortion gives women more control over their lives. It checks the explosive population growth. It is a civil right so deeply engrained in society that the Supreme Court—dominated by reactionaries—would overturn it at its peril, the peril of the Republican Party and the peril to Bush's re-election.

Efforts to ban late-term abortions are underway in Congress even though it is a rare procedure. Only the Supreme Court kept late-term abortions legal by striking down a Nebraska law outlawing them.

Bush is unbelievably antediluvian. Sex is a fact of life. And that fact demands the use of condoms to control unwanted pregnancies, to curb AIDS. As the Times concludes grimly: "Women's constitutional liberty has been threatened, essential reproductive health care has been denied or delayed and some women will needlessly die."

It is obvious that the Bush administration is anti-sex and anti-women. It is also obvious that the administration is violently pro-corporation and pro-money.

Just before Christmas, the top Bush trade negotiator blocked an agreement by the World Trade Organization to provide life-saving drugs to poor countries being ravaged by baby-killing diseases like HIV and malaria.

The agreement would have allowed those countries to use generic drugs at much cheaper cost. But, no, the negotiator cried out, this was "an assault on the intellectual property rights" of drug firms.

To the Bushites money is always more important than people. It's an old, old Republican story. The GOP opposes abortion but abandons children the moment they are born. (Bush's budget for the next fiscal year would slash 33,000 kids from the child care rolls.)

This is a savage, heartless White House.

Sparks Tribune, Feb. 6, 2003

Gay marriages? Yes

One of the huge and ever-lasting problems of democracy is that the majority of people vote with their hearts and not with the their heads. That is why we have such bad laws and such bad politicians.

Politicians cater to the stupidities of the masses. Telling the truth to voters would be fatal to their careers.

Sen. John McCain of Arizona actually opposed flying the Confederate flag over the state capitol in South Carolina. But he told voters otherwise when in ran for president in 2000. Sen. Dick Bryan of Nevada opposed flag-burning—until he was no longer running for office.

Anyway, the nonpoliticking truth is that people should vote no on Question 2 on the Nevada ballot Tuesday. The measure provides that the state constitution be amended to prohibit gay and lesbian marriages.

A bar to gay marriages is discriminatory. Couples of the same sex should have the protections, legal rights and benefits of all Nevadans. Same-sex marriage rights include insurance coverage, visitation to intensive care wards or emergency rooms, medical decisions, child custody and inheritance.

European nations are much more tolerant than so many Americans. In the Netherlands, same-sex marriage couples have full equality, including guidelines for divorce. (Oscar Wilde, in a delicious reversal of the cliché, noted that "divorces are made in heaven.")

Dutch gays and lesbians can adopt children. Denmark allowed gay marriages in 1989. In Norway and Sweden, gay couples can register their unions at city hall. In Germany, gay marriages provide the same inheritance rights as hetrosexual couples.

But in America, intolerance is deep-seated. Sen. Trent Lott of Mississippi calls homosexuality a sin. And a Nevada

Republican says that gays and lesbians who marry must answer to "a higher being."

Yes on fluoride, tobacco

This corner urges a yes vote on WC-1. *Only in Nevada* would it be an issue four decades after most cities have happily fluoridated their water. Fluoride efficacy fighting tooth decay is unquestionable. Former Surgeon General Everett Koop rightly calls fluoridation "the single most important commitment that a community can make to the oral health of its citizens."

Voters are also urged to vote yes on WC-8 attacking the ever-growing public awareness of the perils of secondhand smoke.

Neal for governor

Joe Neal, Democratic candidate for governor, has been denied backing by the state's AFL-CIO. Ditto for another normal supporter of Democrats, the state teacher's union. That makes two good reasons to vote for Neal.

Neal is for people power. His opponent, Gov. Kenny Guinn, is for casino power. Once again, most voters don't know what is good for them.

State Senator Neal has long been the hairshirt of the gambling industry. Why? Because he has had the temerity to urge what the state has long needed to do: increase casino taxes.

Those taxes, the lowest in the world, have not been raised since 1987 and then a paltry one-half of 1 percent. The state population grows incrementally, causing increased demand for state services and straining the budget. Casinos chortle all the way to the bank.

Neal, who is black, has one blind spot: he backs black conservatives for office even when their rivals have liberal credentials. It is reverse racism.

In local races, it would be wise in many cases to vote the opposite of candidates and issues endorsed by the Reno

Gazette-Journal. Examples: it urged a vote against Vivian Freeman in the 24th Assembly district and for Maurice Washington in Senate District 2. That means you should vote for Freeman and Washington's opponent, Joe Carter.

The RGJ says Freeman has "an impressive record" as a veteran assemblywoman. It says her foe, Jason Geddes, faces a "steep learning curve and has much to learn before he can truly be effective." It's the twisted logic of the U.S. Supreme Court.

Freeman has a long liberal record. As for Washington, he's the Nevada equivalent of Justice Clarence Thomas: an Uncle Tom, an Oreo cookie and a reactionary.

Gutless wonder

Frankie Sue Del Papa is not seeking re-election as state attorney general. Good. Not only has she been hostile to the media in her two terms, she's the gutless wonder of Nevada politics. She has feinted toward the governorship and feinted for the U.S. Senate. Both times she "fainted."

Sparks Tribune, Nov. 3, 2002

Canada to dump pot law?

MONTREAL—Most Americans ignore Canada. Oh, Maine seniors often travel to Canada to get prescription drugs far cheaper than they can in America. But the American media set the tone: they mostly ignore Canada.

They shouldn't. Canada has much to teach America. It is a more humane nation. It has national health insurance. America, the wealthiest nation in the world, does not. Canada abolished the death penalty. America has not.

The newspapers here, both in English and French, are more serious, more thoughtful and more profound than most American newspapers. The Globe and Mail and National Post, Canada's two national newspapers, are nearly as good as the New York Times, the best in the world.

The Globe and Mail has wide columns, wonderfully large pictures and uncluttered makeup that make for easy reading. It has good writing and provocative columns. It is everything that the jumbled, spineless and junky newspapers like USA Today and the Reno Gazette-Journal are not.

The latest brouhaha here is over decriminalization of marijuana. Most of the Canadian press seems to be strongly in favor. The Globe and Mail editorialized: "Outdated and ineffectual, our cannabis laws gobble up abnormal amounts of police and court resources and badly need an overhaul. More than 1.5 million Canadians regularly smoke cannabis."

Right on, as the flaming youth of the 1960s used to say.

The Toronto Star weighed in with an editorial supporting reform: "Marijuana remains a (habit), like drinking alcohol or smoking cigarettes. It would be better handled through public education, not by giving people criminal records."

William Johnson, G&M columnist, noted how Canadian police lobbyists routinely put out "grotesque disinformation." He cites scare talk about pot legalization by the Canadian Police Association, which calls the violent crime rate in the Netherlands the highest in Europe. (The enlightened Dutch permit pot smoking in cafes and allow take home of up to five grams of marijuana.)

The facts are otherwise. The United Nations reported that the murder rate per 100,000 is 15.2 percent in America. In Canada it is 2.3 percent and in Holland just 1.8 percent.

Columnist Johnson, urging Canada to modernize its soft drug laws, concluded by citing the film "Traffic" in which the Michael Douglas character, who is in charge of enforcing U.S. drug laws, says that the drug war is essentially a war against America's children.

But such common sense will never influence the drug warriors in America.

Asa Hutchinson, director of the U.S. Drug Enforcement Administration, expressed outrage that Canada was even considering adoption of what he calls a lax policy. Why, he said, U.S. citizens would flock to Canada to smoke pot. Moreover, they would bring the stuff back and hamper "the aggressive U.S. war on drugs."

The absurdity of the Hutchinson view is manifest.

Enlightened nations are concluding that such a bogus war wastes time and money. It locks up nonviolent people who could be a benefit to society and a benefit to themselves. Among the enlightened nations are Britain, Switzerland and Australia.

But no one ever accused the United States of being enlightened.

Unfortunately, the Canadian media are far less progressive about gay marriage. The Ontario Superior Court ruled last month that the traditional definition of marriage, between a man and a woman, is unconstitutional because it violates the equality provision of the Canadian Charter of Rights and Freedoms.

Great. But an editorial in the National Post complained that the ruling by "a handful of unelected judges" is profoundly undemocratic, ignoring the will of the majority of Canadians. The newspaper deplored what it called making law from the bench.

What too many Canadians and too many Americans don't realize is that courts in both countries must guarantee that the tyranny of the majority is not allowed to run roughshod over basic human rights.

For example, had it not been for the U.S. Supreme Court outlawing school segregation, Alabama, Mississippi and South Carolina would probably still have segregated schools today.

The U.S. Senate, so often a cemetery for progressive legislation, is a sad example of relying on popular will to enact needed reforms. The U.S. Supreme Court, for example, had to outlaw the poll tax when the cowardly senators would not.

In short, as I.F. Stone, late, great gadfly journalist, remarked: "If you give power to the people we'd all be in jail."

Sparks Tribune, Aug. 15, 2002

Humane vote on pot

Oregon, the most progressive state in the union, has approved medical marijuana and death-with-dignity laws. Its constitution says that obscenity can neither be prohibited nor censored.

And on Nov. 5 it seeks voter approval of a proposal to provide every Oregon citizen full medical insurance—no copayments and no deductibles. If approved, it would be the first universal health care plan in the nation.

Oregon is far in advance of the federal government, which has no national health plan, no medical marijuana law and no euthanasia law. It is also ahead of a U.S. Supreme Court ruling that allows prosecution of so-called obscenity on the basis of community standards.

Oregon is proving what Justice Louis Brandeis hoped: states can serve as laboratories for needed laws that Congress will not enact.

Nevada too, with its libertarian bent, can be a laboratory for progressive laws. It has legalized prostitution. It was the first state to legalize gambling. It led the way to abandonment of divorce laws and legalized medical marijuana.

Now Nevadans can be pioneers in another progressive measure: voting yes on Question 9 on Nov. 5. The measure would make it legal to possess up to three ounces of marijuana. Approval would make Nevada the first state to legalize cannabis.

It is absurd to make pot smoking a felony. It is no more felonious than alcohol or tobacco, both legal products. Marijuana is not addictive. Cigarettes and liquor are.

Prohibition, from 1919 to 1933, was the worst social experiment the nation ever undertook. Marijuana prohibition has succeeded only in filling the jails, spending billions for enforcement, wasting huge amounts of the productive lives of nonviolent Americans and refusing to ease the pain and suffering of thousands.

Pot remains the thirdmost popular recreational drug, just behind tobacco and alcohol. Its use is no more harmful to society—if you don't drive while high—than social drinking of alcohol. Annual death tally of Americans: alcohol consumption, 100,000. Pot smoking: none.

Cash-strapped Nevada would find marijuana legalization bountiful. One study estimated that a tax on sales of pot could reap $28.6 million yearly.

The government's demonization of pot never did make sense. As the mainstream New England Journal of Medicine puts it: federal policy is "misguided, heavy-handed and inhumane."

Nor, for that matter, does the phony war on drugs make sense. Treatment, not jail, is the answer. Just as drinkers and smokers are not harassed, neither should pot smokers be. One columnist has called such harassment and incarceration "official terrorism."

The bogus war on drugs goes far to make America a police state. This insanity we owe to gutless politicians who want to be perceived as tough on crime—and so they *say* smoking pot is a crime.

The Shafer Commission recommended in 1972 that pot be legalized. But President Nixon and politicans since then have said no. They persist in keeping their heads in the sand while ignoring serious problems in society.

The Unitarian Universalist Church has urged all drugs to be legal with a prescription. Such a progressive policy would take the crime out of drugs, do away with inflated street prices and save billions on drug enforcement.

The federal drug enforcement budget is $20 billion. America spends $50 billion annually on prisons. About one quarter of the 2 million in the drug Gulag need not be there. They are non-violent prisoners.

Britain, more civilized than America, will no longer arrest people who smoke marijuana. The Netherlands, more civilized than America, has legalized pot. Luxembourg, more civilized than America, has ended jail sentence for pot possession.

Spain and Italy, more civilized than America, do not jail people using drugs. Portugal, more civilized than America, has decriminalized drug use.

But in uncivilized America, drug czar John Walters is what Jim Hightower calls the Dr. Strangelove of the stupid drug war. Drug hawk Walters sent U.S. agents to uproot marijuana gardens that are legal for thousands of sick patients in California and to raid cannabis clubs.

Back to the UUs. They have been so often vindicated by history. They fought for black rights before it was popular, urged sex education against howls by conservatives and pushed for a gay clergy and gay marriage.

The UUs are humanists. If the nation and world were constituted like them, it would be a far, far better universe.

Sparks Tribune, Oct. 24, 2002

Clark stutters on gays

Gen. Wesley Clark brings impeccable military credentials to do battle with the reprehensible President Bush. But Clark, who recently joined the crowded field of Democrats seeking to dethrone Bush, is still muddled and befuddled on social issues.

On gays in the military, Clark wishy-washily says: "I'd like to see the military relook the policy. I didn't say change it—I said relook it."

Not good enough. Gays belong in the military without ifs, ands or buts. The don't ask, don't tell policy is discriminatory, wasteful, inhumane—and stupid.

Clark sounds as gutless on the issue as former President Clinton. Clinton campaigned in 1992 with a promise to lift the ban on gays and lesbians in the armed services. But he had barely entered the White House when he surrendered to a military cabal led by Colin Powell, then head of the Joint Chiefs.

Congress came up with what it considered a compromise: the don't-ask policy. It is an embarrassing policy, unworthy of a nation that could be great instead of being just the mightiest.

Under this dreadful policy, the Pentagon purges Arabic language specialists. It fires officers who are superior, intelligent, perceptive, self-reliant, dynamic, personable and with unlimited potential. It cavalierly tosses out about 1,200 gays a year, losing talent and wasting money on extensive training.

Speaking of embarrassment. President Bush is so backward on gayism that he calls it a sin, a violation of "the sanctity of marriage." Traditional marriage is hardly sacred if 50 percent end in divorce. Moreover, marriage is a civic institution not a religious one.

When will the bulk of the American people realize

that gays and lesbians are human beings like heterosexuals? They are entitled to the same civil rights: the right to join the military, the right to marry, the right to adopt children, the right to inherit, the right to hospital visitation and the right to joint insurance policies.

The media tells us about sexual harassment of women in the military, particularly at the Air Force Academy. But they give relatively little coverage of harassment of military gays.

The Christian right is particularly virulent. It asks for gays to save themselves from their "awful, horrible lifestyle." They add that turning to Jesus would set gays free. They promote anti-gay adoption laws throughout the nation, thus denying children wonderful and loving parents.

It is obvious the Christian right knows nothing about Christianity. Indeed, it is the antithesis of Christianity.

But even a rational religious group, the Episcopalians, has been riven by the election of a gay bishop and approval by the Episcopal general convention. It is hard to avoid the impression that so many religious groups are irreligious.

Civil union for gays is legal in Vermont. Former Gov. Howard Dean, signing civil union into law, made the valid declaration: "Those of us who came to age during the civil rights movement have long understood that the strength of America lies in its commitment to equal rights under the law for everyone."

Sadly, the Republican leadership indulges in violent anti-gayism. Pennsylvanian Rick Santorum, No. 3 in the Senate, absurdly links homosexuality with bigamy, polygamy, adultery and incest. Yet, Bush lauds Santorum as "an inclusiveness man." Tom DeLay, pest exterminator become House majority leader, lauds Santorum's "courage." Bill First, Senate majority leader, seeks a constitutional amendment barring gay marriages.

Florida, Mississippi and Utah forbid adoptions by

same-sex couples. Florida's ban was upheld by a federal judge two years ago, accepting the state's bogus argument that men and women couples provide a more stable home for kids.

Studies show that gay and lesbian parents try to be supermoms and dads, far more than hetrosexual couples. They make tremendous efforts to keep their kids happy and secure.

A state judge in Hawaii wrote in 1996 that "the single most important factor in the development of a happy, healthy and well-adjusted child is the nurturing relationship between parents and child."

That correct conclusion has nothing to do with whether parents are gay or lesbian. In Florida, one quarter of the children adopted annually go to heterosexual single parents. Florida law assures that some kids will not be adopted into loving, caring homes.

Meanwhile, the world has a showcase, humane society in the Netherlands. Eight percent of marriages are between same-sex partners. Indeed, the Dutch have become so blasé about it that some same-sex marriages end in divorce—and court-ordered alimony.

Sparks Tribune, Oct. 9, 2003

Canada shames America

Canadians can't quite believe it. Suddenly we're interesting.
Naomi Klein, The Nation columnist

It speaks ill of this backward nation when tradition-bound, reserved and conservative Canada is far more liberal on three important social issues: gay marriage, marijuana and hard drugs.

Canada has legalized same-sex weddings, decriminalized marijuana and opened a safe drug injection center in Vancouver, British Columbia. The United States is not just retrograde on these matters. It is often cruel, heartless—and ostrich-like.

Few seem to be complaining in Canada about measures that would cause a furor in the United States. As Canadian Prime Minister Jean Chrétien wisely said of gay marrige: society is constantly evolving.

Unfortunately, not in the United States. America is puritanical and purblind. On the drug war, for example, it refuses to accept the truth: it is a fiasco. The war is tremendously costly. And it has done no more than propel prison warehousing to 2.1 million. (More than 500,000 prisoners have been committed for pot possession.)

The drug war was a failure from the start three decades ago when Gov. Nelson Rockefeller pushed though punitive anti-drug laws in New York. Presidents Reagan, Bush I, Clinton and Bush II all have backed the bogus drug war because it is a big vote-getter.

Yet all of Canada's progressivism on drugs makes the regressive Bush administration quiver with indignation. Its drug czar, the reprehensible John Walters in the reprehensible Bush administration, vows to "respond to the threat."

The U.S. government heartlessly escalates its asinine drug war to medical pot users like Californian Valerie Corral. She smokes marijuana because it is the only way she can ease the pain of epileptic seizures and excruciating headaches. Thugs from the Drug Enforcement Agency crashed into her legal marijuana hospice with flak jackets and automatic weapons—all at 3:30 a.m. as if she were a terrorist. A paraplegic patient in the hospice, unable to stand, was handcuffed in her bed.

Compassionate conservatism? Attorney General John Ashcroft sent his minions into California to arrest an Oakland man, Ed Rosenthal, who was carrying out that mandate of the people to allow medical marijuana.

At Rosenthal's trial in federal court, the judge refused to allow testimony that he was working for Oakland under California's Compassionate Use Act of 1996, which allows pot cultivation for medical marijuana.

He was convicted. Only after the verdict did the jurors learn that what Rosenthal was doing was legal in California. Five jurors were so enraged that they held a press conference to apologize to Rosenthal and denounce a legal system the allows such an injustice.

What is also odious about the drug policy is locking up non-violent, intelligent people who could be so productive to society. Each prisoner in the American Gulag, as a former prisoner friend rightly called the bursting U.S. jails, costs the federal government $30,000 a year.

Drug users simply do not belong in jail. In the drug war, arrests, prosecution and jailings cost $40 billion annually, much of it for senseless prosecution of harmless pot smokers, plant growers and dealers.

What this country desperately needs is to treat drug addiction more like an illness than a crime as California has done. It desperately needs to decriminalize pot, which would allow medical use of marijuana that nine states have approved.

And it needs some of the humaneness and understanding of Quebec's highest court when it ruled last summer: "Same-sex couples are capable of forming long, lasting, loving and intimate relationships."

No, marijuana use does not lead to harder drugs. Study after study proves it. Worldwide medical literature also demonstrates that marijuana meets a medical need.

Another evil associated with the bogus drug war is civil asset forfeiture. DEA agents and police can seize and keep as much property as they want without due process of law, without reimbursement—and even in cases without a conviction.

In America, two potent drugs are legal: tobacco and alcohol. But insignificant hemp is illegal though it has less than 1 percent of the THC chemical that gives pot its zip.

Dutch druggists can sell pot to patients with nausea or who are suffering from pain caused by cancer, AIDS or multiple sclerosis. Safe-injection programs are legal in the Netherlands, Switzerland and Australia. Belgium and the Netherlands pioneered in legal gay unions.

Such nations are humane. The United States is not.

Sparks Tribune, Oct. 2, 2003

People and Places

English cathedrals

YORK, England—Three great cathedrals in Europe are Notre-Dame in Paris, Chartres in France and St. Paul's in London. Notre-Dame is famous for its marvelous flying buttresses and fascinating gargoyles, Chartres its magnificent stained glass and St. Paul's for its soaring dome.

But a recent visit to York makes you wonder: is the York Minster more impressive than those three? The Minster is gigantic, wide and long—and yet simple in its grandeur. It has graceful, unadorned lines. Even on an overcast day it seems to glow as if lit. In contrast, Chartres is dark and gloomy. Notre-Dame and St. Paul's are too encrusted with statues, tombs and relics.

At the head of the nave in the Minster hangs, dramatically, a huge, plain wooden cross drapped with a pure white, silken cloth. In the north transcept is the Five Sisters Window, beautiful with grey-green glass. Then another beauty: a rose window in the south transcept. And still another: the Great West Window painted in 1338, called the heart of Yorkshire because of its heart-shaped tracery.

The awe was enhanced by the choir rehearsing for evensong, a wonderful tradition in Anglican churches. The choir master, garbed in red, abruptly stopped the choir with an impatient gesture. He wanted the full-throated joy that Thomas Hardy wrote of in his poem, "The Darkling Thrush." The choir reached the glorious heights on its second try.

My wife, Mary, took communion in the Minster. It was a moving moment to see her walk up the aisle. I thought that the eucharist would never again be quite the same for her as it was in this great cathedral.

The Minister provides a wonderful postcard and photo background for a walk around the medieval walls of York. From those walls, what Bardolator could resist reciting

Richard's opening speech from "Richard III": "Now is the winter of our discontent made glorious summer by this sun of York"?

About 200 miles to the southwest lies Bath. It boasts my favorite street in the world: the semi-circular Royal Crescent, the marvelously engineered Roman baths and the Bath Abbey with its delightful fallen angel on the facade, plunging down Jacob's ladder.

Continuing on the cathedral trail, we visited Winchester Cathedral in southern England. It pales in comparison with the Minster. Jane Austen is buried here. So is Izaak Walton, patron saint of fishermen. It also has a memorial to Samuel Wilberforce, bishop of Winchester in the 1870s who valiantly fought slavery.

In the cathedral a small group of school children were making clay gargoyles. The kids were deadly earnest in their instructive play, so fresh-faced, so angelic in their innocence. I recalled the Jesus injunction: "Suffer the little children to come unto me…"

The countryside around Winchester is "profound England" just as there is a "profound France," the deep, abiding countryside far from the madding cities. Here there are tall hedges, shady woodlands, streams, country lanes. And greenery everywhere, pleasing a visitor from Nevada where brown predominates.

Here there is the sweet song of England's blackbird, a *turdus* like the American robin with the same mannerisms and delicious song. ("A Midsummer Night's Dream": "the ousel cock so black of hue, with orange-tawny bill.") Here the turtle dove coos incessantly its "tour-ter-elles, tour-ter-elles, tour-ter-elles."

Walking around typical Hampshire country in south England, you see a 16th century Tudor timbered house. Not far away you encounter a *10th century* Saxon stone church. Churchyard gravestones are moss-covered, the weathered stones reminding you of Gray's "Elegy Written in a Country Churchyard" at Stoge Poges, England.

In London, about 50 miles to the east of Winchester, a boy stood on the gravestone of Oliver Cromwell in the Westminster Abbey, oblivious of the history of the Lord Protector. *Sic semper gloria mundi.* A large floor placard honored the burial site of Darwin, flooding me with thoughts of the Galapagos and the fact of evolution.

The poets' corner pays homage to Shakespeare, history's greatest writer, and to Longfellow, my boyhood favorite. I was surprised and delighted to find a "leftists' corner" in the hallowed Westminster Abbey near the Churchill memorial. Among socialists buried here is Clement Atlee, who as prime minster after World War II brought national health to Britain.

For the secular visitor, the cathedrals of England are marvels of medieval architecture. For theists, they make them feel the presence of God.

Sparks Tribune, June 19, 2003

Homelessness and mummery

LONDON—Observations and reflections on a recent visit to England:

I was astonished to see entrances to Parliament, seat of the oldest democracy in the world, barricaded with huge concrete blocks. But even more astonishing was to see police at the entrances carrying menacing automatic weapons. It was sad—but all too necessary after 9/11.

• Orwell ! Thou shouldst be living at this hour: London hath need of thee: she is a fen of the homeless. An update of Orwell's "Down and Out in Paris and London" is needed because the homeless are evident today in this teeming city.

Near Marble Arch at dusk, a couple of homeless sat on cardboard while pulling on sleeping bags. And in St. Martin's-in-the-Fields off Trafalgar Square, a homeless woman had a black cloth pulled over her eyes so she could sleep in a pew. In another pew, a homeless man slept.

The church attracts the homeless because it is a warm, safe haven. Indeed, the church has become such a favorite place for the homeless that authorites have had to close the church an hour before concerts and services.

A church flyer notes: "For some time we have been experiencing difficulties with a number of people effectively 'camping' in the church for the entire day, day after day…On occasions such people fall asleep for hours. Then they are aggressive toward staff when they are awakened and asked to leave because the building is closing."

• The mummery of the monarchy continues despite the scandals and wasted money. Yes, yes, it's British tradition. Yes, yes, it's good for gawking tourists and the tourist trade. But it has no place in a democracy. America and France had the good sense to abolish royalty two centuries ago.

The Scottish Socialist Party, republican to the core,

was right to boycott a recent speech by Queen Elizabeth II at the start of a new session of the Scots parliament. The leader of the party promised to fight for "an independent socialist Scotland, a socialist republic, a Scotland of citizens not a Scotland of subjects." Hear! Hear!

• And speaking of nonsenical traditions. In a procession of town fathers and mothers to the Bath Abbey, the judges wore those silly wigs that Chief Justice John Marshall rightly abolished in 1803 for the U.S. Supreme Court.

• Globalization is inevitable. But it is still dismaying to see England packed with McDonald's, Starbucks, Burger Kings and KFCs. Such firms are about as English as Patty's pig.

• Some areas of Highgate Cemetery in London have deteriorated terribly. Broken gravestones, weeds- and vine-choked gravestones and overgrown plots. But the Marx grave site is well-tended, drawing fresh flowers from Britons and worshipers visiting from around the world.

Carved in gold on the huge tombstone, topped by a burly bust of Marx, are the stirring words of history's greatest economist: "Philosophers have only interpreted the world in various ways. The point, however, is to change it."

• The Guardian is the best newspaper in Britain. It reads like The Nation, a liberal-to-radical magazine in America. The Guardian is leftish and angry—as it should be. Its columnists are nearly always worth reading. Its editorials first-rate.

The paper attacks wars, wrongs and injustices of the Blair and Bush administrations. The Guardian is rightly pro-euro, pro-European and anti-corporation. Unfortunately, 75 percent of the British people read the tabloids and trash papers of right-wing owners like Rupert Murdoch and Conrad Black.

• The view of the dome inside St. Paul's is badly disfigured with scaffolding necessitated by renovation. I had the same ill luck visiting Rome decades ago. The Sistine

Chapel was closed for the cleaning of Michelangelo's incredible ceiling.

Nevertheless, I've always liked the comment of Christopher Wren, architect of St. Paul's. The Latin phrase is embedded in gold beneath the dome: "*Si monumentum requiris circumspice.*" (If you seek my monument, look about you.")

• A visit to Shakespeare's Globe reconstructed at Bankside thrilled this Bardolator. I shall always recall this sacred place when I see "Henry V": "May we cram within this wooden O the very casques that did affright the air at Agincourt?"

During a tour, we watched a rehearsal for "Richard III." It was fascinating to observe the players stop, procede, confer with the director. Sitting on those wooden benches close to where the groundlings stood, I felt as if I was truly communing with the great Shakespeare.

Sparks Tribune, June 26, 2003

Quebec: very French

QUEBEC—A columnist in the Toronto Globe and Mail recently wrote that just two cities in North America, Montreal and San Francisco, could belong in Europe. He was wrong.

San Francisco is the best city in America. It is the most progressive. It is blessed by geography and packed with culture. But it is not European. Quebec is.

This tourist spent five days recently in Quebec and felt all the time he was in France. The French language and French culture are pervasive. Plus: the narrow, colorful streets carry an undeniable Old World flavor.

Indeed, in two ways Quebec is more civilized than France. Quebec sidewalks are free of the disgusting dog crap found in France and its best restaurants are free of obnoxious smoking.

As for the justly celebrated French gastronomy, it is no myth. You feel as if dinners in Quebec were prepared just for you.

The food is not only delicious but appears on the plate as almost too beautiful to eat. At one restaurant in Quebec my wife had *foie gras* as an appetitzer. On the plate was a shiny red apple sculpted in the form of a beautiful swan. *Parfait*, as the French say. My veal filet, surrounded by vegetables, looked—and tasted—magnificent.

No blaring, obnoxious rock music. Just softly playing classical music. Conversation. Plenty of time between courses. Good wine. In short, civilized dining.

One drawback to paradise in the Quebec area is the tours. A Gray Line trip to Ste-Anne-de-Beaupré, worldwide pilgrimage site 20 miles east of Quebec, takes five hours in a visit that should be half that time.

Why? Because the tour made gratituous stops at places

like a copper factory and a bread and honey shop. Gullible tourists buy, proving lucrative for both the merchants and the tour operators. But it's a waste of precious touring time.

The basilica at Ste-Anne is dedicated to the mother of the Virgin Mary. Tucked away in one corner near the front of the basilica is a collection of crutches and braces, supposedly thrown away by "cured" invalids. It reminded this visitor of the crutches above the grotto at Lourdes, another hugely popular pilgrimage site in France.

A special exhibition of Bourdelle, French sculptor (1861-1929), was showing at the Quebec art museum. About his panels for a theater in Paris, Bourdelle wrote: "All my muses at the theater are gestures captured from the flights of Isadora Duncan (celebrated dancer)."

Significant was what Bourdelle told his art students: "I want you to put more than physical effort into your work. I want you to invest your mind too. Do not copy me. Sing your own song."

It is similar to the words Whitman penned in "Leaves of Grass." He gives poet-teacher advice to his students and acolytes: "He that by me spreads a wider breast than my own, proves the width of my own / He most honors my style who learns under it to destroy the teacher."

Trains run regularly between Montreal and Quebec. (The pleasure of train travel is a reminder of how sad it would be if America lets Amtrak die.) Train travel has one problem: people on cellphones. A guy behind us on one trip talked interminably—and annoyingly. Sometimes ever-advancing technology is not progress.

In Montreal, the art museum is one of the finest in the world. The building on Sherbrooke street reminded me of the Pompidou museum of modern art in Paris with its exterior glass.

The galleries are uncluttered, presenting the art in an attractive way. (Unlike the terribly cluttered Soames museum in London with its priceless Hogarths almost hidden amid the jumble.)

The permanent collection at the Montreal gallery is a feast. El Greco's "Ecstasy of St. Francis" shines across the room. Grey. White hand with long, delicate fingers. Stigmata. Furry garment with hood. I pulled up an arm chair in front of the work, feeling lucky to be contemplating great art.

(Question: why is that art galleries throughout the world seldom have postcards in their book shops of works you have just seen and cherish? The El Greco, for example.)

Too many people saunter through the galleries, failing to scrutinize the art works. I recall newspaper days in Baltimore when, visiting one gallery, a woman said to me sternly:

"Young man, you must study paintings. Look intensely at every corner. Look high, look low, look at the middle. Look *all* over."

Sound advice.

Sparks Tribune, Aug. 22, 2002

.

University autocrat stifles dissent

John Mackay fixes a firm gaze on the Comstock about 25 miles southeast in Virginia City where he made millions in silver mining. He leans lightly on a pick in his left hand, his right hand cupping a mineral rock. His sleeves are rolled up, collar open, his mustache seeming to bristle.

One thing is missing: duct tape over his mouth.

A mouth-taped Mackay statue facing the quad at the University of Nevada, Reno would symbolize the firing of Jane Long as dean of the Mackay School of Mines. Her crime? She had the effrontery to oppose the UNR reorganization plan that would bury the school in a proposed science college.

The Mackay statue, sculpted by Gutzon Borglum whose gigantic presidential heads adorn Mount Rushmore in South Dakota, is a monument to the national and international renown of the mining school. It symbolizes Nevada's historic mining past—and its future.

John Louie, seismology professor who represents the Mackay school on the Faculty Senate, put it well: "The most widely known brand name in the entire university." This is the brand name that the UNR President John Lilley would obliterate.

But the most terrible thing about the Long affair is the stifling of free speech. Lilley sent his hatchetman and sycophant, Provost John Frederick, to deliver the blow to the First Amendment and to academia. (Those wondering why UNR needed a provost now know.)

Aside from being an autocrat, Lilley is also a hypocrite. In an email message to the university community after the firing, he paid homage to the First Amendment: "The freedom to dissent is central to the life of the university." It sure is. But one sentence later Lilley added: "Faculty members at this university will

96

not suffer administrative repercussions for their exercise of free expression."

Tell that to Jane Long.

The Ad Hoc Committee of the Faculty Senate also reached Long's conclusion. "No evidence is provided from similar institutions, from detailed cost comparisons or even from relevant theoretical models of management and organization that guide us in understanding how *this type* of reorganization...addresses the issues we face," the committee reported.

Those issues: a crying need for many more professors, huge enrollment growth, insufficient support personnel and serious need for more office, research and classroom space.

The lightly credentialed Lilley came to UNR in 2001 from Penn State-Erie only after the Board of Regents rejected a faculty committee's first choice. The Regents obviously picked him because he would be more malleable. (A Penn State source, who watched Lilley at work, recalled him as arrogant, a man who considered himself far more important than he was.)

Lilley sought to make an immediate splash rather than getting the lay of the land for a year as a wiser man would have done. He was determined to split the College of Arts and Science in two. It was such a bad idea that A&S dean, Robert Mead, resigned over the issue.

Another bad Lilley move early in his reign was to issue an edict allowing athletes to register before other students. Never mind that the Faculty Senate had rejected the idea.

One bad Lilley idea deserves another: turning UNR into a research university. Research is essential for academicians. But it is hardly the primary mission of land-grant UNR.

Lilley keeps talking about taking UNR to the next level, as if it were a junior college when he arrived. Then another bad idea from the Lilley administration: tearing down the planetarium, replacing it with a parking lot. It was not just bad PR. It was a stupid.

During the uproar, outrage and disruption caused by the reorganization plan, Regent Howard Rosenberg continued his longtime sellout. Rosenberg, a UNR art professor, started out as a Regent vowing to speak for students and faculty. Now he is just a mouthpiece for the administration.

Rosenberg said of Jane Long: "She works for the administration. It has every reason to expect a certain amount of discretion and loyalty." In other words, UNR is a corporation, hostile to all ideas and particularly hostile to contrarian ones.

Lilley seems to be the type who will brook no opposition. He seems as determined to adopt the reorganization plan—whatever the Faculty Senate decides—as President Bush is to make war in Iraq.

Sparks Tribune, Feb. 27, 2003

Gauguin's Tahiti

TAHITI, French Polynesia—This is still the land of Gauguin and the people he painted: the ever-present flower behind the ear, the colorful cloth wrapped around the body as skirt, dress or shorts, and the morose faces of women.

But even when Gauguin first came here in 1891, Tahiti was no longer paradise. He complained that this storied South Pacific island was already French, that all the ancient ways were disappearing and that the missionaries were "sweeping away part of the poetry."

Missionaries were horrified by Tahitians surfing in the nude. They also condemned tattooing as "a morally dangerous glorification of the sinful body." Fortunately, the Polynesians ignored their strictures. Tattooing is still prevalent today among men and women.

Melville, author of "Moby Dick," also complained about the missionaries. Coming here in the 1840s, Melville asked why the natives should be forced into an alien church, bow to a foreign government and to adopt alien ways.

Why indeed. It is the height of presumptuousness for missionaries to impose their religion—their false beliefs— on native peoples, to foist on them their puritanical notions.

As for government, the Polynesians are an overseas territory of France. They are represented in the National Assembly and the Senate. But that is not enough. Nationalistic fervor is growing. An opposition political party is pledging "economic, social, cultural and political emancipation."

A spur to independence came in 1995 with demonstrations and rioting in Papeete, the capital of Tahiti, over French nuclear testing at atolls southeast of Tahiti, Mururoa and Fangataufa.

Back to Gauguin. In his fanciful, fictional and plagiarized memoir of Tahiti, "Noa Noa" (fragrance), the artist exulted that he escaped from "bourgeois France." He "went native," barefooted, his body "almost always naked" and bronzed by the sun. He took a *vahine* (woman) to live with him, becoming "carefree, calm and loving."

But if Gauguin was disappointed in Tahiti, so is the Gauguin museum here disappointing. It is informational, with many storyboards and artifacts, but little of Gauguin's art.

One wall is full of Gauguins but, alas, all reproductions. One of my Gauguin favorites pictured here is "Nevermore," a homage to Edgar Allan Poe. It shows a nude Polynesian woman lying on her stomach with a raven perched on a window ledge.

Personally, I'm not fond of Gauguin. Perhaps it's because his women are unattractive: big hips, big thighs, splayed feet. Still, it's hard to resist a slogan on one of his wood carvings: "Soyez amoureuses (et) vous serez heureuses." (Be amorous and you will be happy.)

One of most interesting things in Tahiti is a brightly color piece of wraparound cloth, the pareu (par-ay-you). Five or six feet long, it can be made into a wide variety of garments. Another fascination: a dance similar to the Hawaiian hula. The erotic hip-swinging is barely noticeable. What is memorable are the gentle hand and arm gestures, the happy smiles.

As for the singing musicians, their driving beat, toe-tapping music gets to you. They seem to be making love with their voices, their instruments. The music is a combination of rock, French pop tunes and Polynesian songs. Their happiness is infectious.

The Polynesian *joie de vivre* is also evident in their dancing: so rhythmic, with dips, sways, swings, swirls. Polynesians dance with such feeling, such soul. They seem most happy when dancing.

Tahiti is "a land more passing fair," as James Hall, co-author of "Mutiny on the Bounty," wrote in a poem. Its volcanic peaks are covered with lush greenery. Coconut palms are everywhere, looking like Hollywood scenery.

Flowers dominate. A profusion of colorful tropical plants line roadways. The vanilla-scented tiare (hibiscus blossom) is ubiquitious: on a plate at bars, behind the ear. Flowers abound in hotel lobbies and hotel rooms.

Tahiti and its northern "suburb," the island of Moorea, lie about 16 degrees below the equator. The humidity is extremely high. Rain is constant. But 30 minutes after a downpour the sun shines.

Because of high tariffs and the whopping cost of transporting goods, it is frightfully expensive here. The daily international Herald Trib costs $4.50.

One caution: the roads around the two islands are hazardous: dogs, motor scooters, bicyclists, potholed roads. People walking along the narrow road, people talking in knots beside the road. Then tropical rainstorms. Driving these roads may be the longest short drives you'll ever take.

Sparks Tribune, Jan. 30, 2003

'Socialist' owners win!

Socialism triumphed over capitalism in a bizarre twist: baseball owners were the socialists and the union the capitalists. Management wanted to share the wealth. The union wanted a free market to get maximum salaries.

Fortunately, the owners got in the recent agreement what is so essential: a measure of competitive balance.

The baseball union is not a classic union in the sense of fighting for the underdogs against mercenary capitalism. It is not negotiating for underpaid coal miners. It is negotiating for millionaires. (Fans naturally react angrily when Alex Rodriquez of the Texas Rangers earns $25 million a year, more than most fans earn in a lifetime.)

The agreement transfers money from rich teams to poorer teams through revenue-sharing and luxury taxes—a good thing. The New York Yankees, with their big bucks, usually buy the pennant and World Series.

The Yankees lure star players like Jason Giambi from the Oakland A's by paying him $11 million a year versus the $4 million he was getting from the A's. They get ace pitcher Mike Mussina by paying him three times as much as the Baltimore Orioles could afford.

And the Yankees do this *ad nauseam*. They have huge TV revenues small-market teams do not. Nine-tenths of the low-market teams have no chance even before spring training begins.

The Pittsburgh Pirates have a payroll $92 million less than the Yankees. The new agreement will have hundreds of millions of dollars going from the Yankees to teams like the Pirates.

But baseball still needs a salary cap that professional football and basketball have. In pro football you have revenue sharing and easier schedules for teams with losing records. Losing teams draft first. You have such great parity that four different teams won the Super Bowl in the past four seasons.

It is that kind of balance that the agreement will partially rectify— partially because the rich Yankees and the wealthy Atlanta Braves will nearly always be contenders.

Siding with fat-cat ballplayers, who make an average of $2.4 million a year, is difficult. And it is difficult to side with the multimillionaire owners who plead poverty while getting taxpayers to build their stadiums. But the owners are right to seek a more level playing field.

Jim Bunning, Hall of Fame pitcher who is now senator from Kentucky, rightly says: "Money does not win games. Teams with the biggest payrolls do not always grab the pennant. But, over time, it is indisputable that big-market teams have an edge over small-market teams."

Yes, teams like the New York Mets will still make dumb personnel decisions like overpaying fat, over-the-hill players. And, yes, low-payroll teams like the Oakland A's will be stunningly successful. (The A's are 27th of 30 franchises in payrolls. Their payroll is one third of the Yankees.)

Why do the A's do well? They have in Billy Beane one of the best general managers in baseball. He has drafted wisely, traded shrewdly and developed an excellent farm system. As one A's player says, Beane has "one of the great minds in baseball."

Steroids: Head in Sand

Unfortunately, baseball refuses to face up to its steroid problem. The new pact calls for surveys and random testing—all bark but no bite.

Estimates of steroid use range from 20 percent to 40 percent. Sports Illustrated, the bible of the sporting world, noted in a June 3 article that steroids are rampant in baseball.

Ken Caminiti, formerly of the San Diego Padres, admitted he took steroids in 1996 when he won the National

League's Most Valuable Player award. Former slugger Jose Canseco admitted using steroids.

The union heretofore has resisted fighting the epidemic. Yet ballplayers are bulking up with steroids while developing potato heads. This makes them susceptible to muscle tears, strained hamstrings and ruptured tendons.

Barry Bonds, San Francisco Giants superman, has denied use of steroids. But he falls under suspicion. As Sports Illustrated writes:

Bonds grew "from a lithe, 185-pound leadoff hitter into a 230-pound force who is one of the greatest home run hitters of all time…Bonds' most dramatic size gains have come in the past four years over which he had doubled his home run rate."

Bonds says he has bulked up by weightlifting. And suspicion is hardly conviction. But the baseball union by its resistance to steroid testing is playing the traditional capitalist role of making money at the expense of justice and fairness.

Sparks Tribune, Sept. 12, 2002

Everywhere but U.S.

VANCOUVER, British Columbia—The philosopher Heidegger wrote contemptuously in 1936 that people would "die of emptiness" if they didn't have what he called the distractions of "the cinema, the radio, the newspaper, the theater, concerts, boxing bouts and travel."

Yet the double-domed sage regularly watched the German soccer team on TV. Well into his eighties, Heidegger loved to demonstrate the soccer moves of the German star Franz Beckenbauer.

Even philosophers cannot resist the World Cup. It is a religion throughout the globe although a religion little practiced in the United States, the land of football, baseball and basketball.

A column appearing in the National Post, one of two national daily newspapers in Canada, put the World Cup in perspective for a visiting American. The columnist, George Johnson of the Calgary Herald, wrote:

"The World Cup of soccer is one championship that is uniquely, truly global. More people play the game than any other. More people will watch this event than any other, including the Olympic Games. An estimated 3 billion viewers will sit in front of their television sets…

"The chronic North American complaint about soccer is a lack of scoring. (But) patience is hardly a hallmark of our lifestyle…Part of the beauty of soccer is that it can be played and mastered by an average-sized person…It has a purity of line, a basic simplicity that renders it accessible to all."

As if to prove his point, teams from the two countries hosting the quadrennial World Cup, Japan and South Korea, advanced to the second round despite the fact that their opponents were bigger and stronger.

Soccer is what Pelé, the Brazilian soccer great of yesteryear, rightly labeled the beautiful game.

Soccer, called football outside the United States, is fascinating. The play is constant, having none of the commercial interruptions that irritate and stretch American sports events on TV to an almost unbearable three hours.

The game often lends itself to multiculturism. The French team that won the World Cup in 1998 included North Africans, West Indians, Africans below the Sahara and Frenchmen.

And as for multiculturalism, Vancouver and Victoria here in British Columbia have been peopled by immigrants long before the word multiculturism became common linguistic currency. It is a polyglot province but a Tower of Babel in which everyone also speaks English.

The two cities abound in Asiatics: Chinese, Japanese, Vietnamese, Thais. They have many Indians and Pakistanis. Portuguese and Spanish are spoken here. Greek and French too.

The shining example of multiculturalism in British Columbia is finding less and less favor in Europe. Denmark, once an immigrant haven, has ended its liberal policy. A new law will prevent all but a few foreigners from settling there—a racist and embarrassing law.

Down with the Queen

The papers and telly have been full of the nonsense about Queen Elizabeth celebrating her Golden Jubilee. Longevity for a *roi fainéant* is no cause for celebration. The monarchy is a vestigal organ, something the French wisely abolished more than two centuries ago.

Yet Canada, like Australia, continues to pay homage to obsolete royalty. It puts the face of the queen on its coins. It is high time that Canada realizes that it is Canada, by God, and cuts the cord to Great Britain. Even the wax museum in Vancouver is overloaded with the sickening royals. (Nearly all of German origin, by the way.)

If Britain's Labor Party had any guts it would abolish

the monarchy as every bit as absurd as fox hunting. (Fox hunting was memorably described by Oscar Wilde as the "unspeakable in pursuit of the uneatable.")

Yes, the monarchy and its trappings are good for the tourists trade. Yes, the monarchy is good for people who want to worship royals as divinities. But like the wigs still worn in British courts, it's silly in the 21st century. (The great Chief Justice of the United States, John Marshall, knew better. He refused to wear a wig when he joined the Supreme Court in 1801.)

Bush the Hypocrite

His Fraudulency, U.S. President Bush, is a dedicated free trader, an exponent of open markets—except when he is playing politics. He recently imposed a 27.2 percent increase on duty for Canadian softwood—a blatant effort to win votes for Republicans in the Pacific Northwest.

Bush did the same thing with steel, hiking tariffs on imports to win GOP votes in battleground states like Pennsylvania. To reap the farm vote for the GOP in rural regions, he signed into law huge, unconscionable subsidies.

Sparks Tribune, June 13, 2002

Blair fumbles euro

LONDON—It was a classic headline in the London Times: "Fog Over Channel; Continent Cut Off." Not Britain cut off, no. Europe.

The headline of yesteryear illustrates the insular attitude of Great Britain. That sense of pride and independence still prevails. Britain refuses to admit that it is in Europe, that its future, economically and politically, is in Europe.

Britain is long overdue to abandon that insularity and adopt the euro, the common currency of 12 European nations. It would spell greater trade, greater investment and a greater number of jobs. It would mean a greater economic gain for Britain.

Chris Patten, a Brit who is a European Union official, backs the euro with philosophy: "The decision on whether Britain should embrace the euro is much more than an economic one. It is an existential choice that will decide Britain's geo-strategic position for years to come."

Former Prime Minister Edward Heath, urging adoption of the euro, says Britain will head "toward the exit door from the EU" if it fails to scrap the pound. And Peter Mandelson, Labor member of Parliament, adds that if Britain spurns the euro it will suffer loss of political influence in Europe, unable "to shape crucial decisions that affect Britain directly."

Such persuasive arguments have not moved the Hamletish Tony Blair, prime minister of Great Britain. He has long been a Europeanist. He is obsessed with his place in history. But that history will speak ill of him if he fails to get the euro adopted. He was elected in 1997 with an overwhelming Labor Party mandate and a promise to decide on the euro.

Four years later he was re-elected, vowing to decide

on the euro in two years. Last month he unveiled a new position: wait-and-see. Oh, and perhaps a referendum. His procrastination is disgraceful.

Hugo Young, Guardian columnist, calls this nondecision "an epitaph on six years of timidity, deception and failure" while the Financial Times laments "Britain's six wasted years of euro indecision."

The Guardian rightly blames Blair: "He missed his European opportunities. He snuggled up to George Bush, fell out with France and Germany, encouraged divisions within the EU and permitted Chancellor George Brown to set the terms of the euro debate."

Blair once had the authority to convince reluctant Britons that their future lies with Europe. But he equivocated. Now it may be too late to mount a successful campaign for the euro.

Europohobia, inflamed and distorted by the right-wing press, and Euroscepticism are growing. Blair lost much popularity and credibility by supinely following Bush to war in Iraq. His credibility was further eroded by the inability to find Iraqi weapons of mass destruction.

Meanwhile, "the British European cause is in tatters," the London Times noted recently. Again because of Blair's procrastinating. Blair himself has attacked "self-mutilating Euroscepticism" so his failure of political nerve is glaring.

Many Brits see the pound as an emblem of nationhood. They argue that its loss would be surrendering sovereignty to continental Europe. Nonsense. The extensive right wing in Britain raises the specter of "the tyranny of Brussels." More nonsense. The EU can only make Britain conform to civil liberties and human rights, to fairness and justice.

Jean Monnet had the magnificent vision of a United States of Europe. Thanks to that vision, the European Community was created in 1957. Then de Gaulle rightly talked of Europe extending from the Atlantic to the Urals.

Europe also extends to Britain. Albion should adopt the constitution of the European Union without quibble. But it should insist that the word God is not included. The EU constitution should remain the strictly humanistic document it is in draft.

As the Guardian put it in an editorial about the constitution: "It spells out exactly the rights that most people in modern societies would regard as both decent and basic. It sets out human dignities and freedoms that are the foundations of a liberal society. It enumerates principles of equality, solidarity and justice that would threaten only the bigot, the thief and the tyrant."

John Donne wrote: "No man is an island, entire of itself; every man is a piece of the continent." Great Britain *is* an island but it is not "entire of itself." It is part of Europe. Its future lies with the euro and the EU.

Sparks Tribune, July 3, 2003

Chaplin: laughs amid cyborg satire

VANCOUVER, British Columbia—The idea that human beings are machines is an old one.

The incomparable Charlie Chaplin played on that theme in "Modern Times," a 1936 film that still elicits gusts of laughter while making the satiric point. Chaplin gets deranged as he tightens bolts furiously in a factory assembly line.

Then he sees an office woman walking by with black buttons on the back of her skirt that look like bolts to be tightened. Outside the plant, Chaplin spots a bosomy woman with black bolts on her breasts.

The sequence is shown again and again at the Vancouver Art Gallery at an exhibition, "The Uncanny Experiments in Cyborg Culture." A signboard notes that the Chaplin film is a cautionary tale about the Industrial Age's threat to control mankind.

A short film by the artist Fernand Léger at the exhibit makes the same point more somberly. It shows a washerwoman repeatedly trudging up steps from the Seine in Paris while hauling a heavy load of laundry.

The weariness on the woman's face calls to mind the Greek myth of Sisyphus, who is eternally condemned to roll a boulder to the top of a hill only to have it roll down again.

Older visitors are delighted to see Rube Goldberg contraptions showing complex solutions to simple tasks. Goldberg was what a storyboard called a "social critic with a piercing vision of modern daily life."

At the end of the exhibit is a cyberbar where kids could design their own cyborg, much like the wonderful hand-to-paw children's zoos for feeding and touching.

Vancouver and Victoria, the two jewel cities of British Columbia, are well worth a visit by American tourists. Among other attractions in Vancouver is the Museum of

Anthropology. Visitors are greeted by huge totem poles produced by aboriginals of British Columbia.

Grotesque. Strange images. They remind one visitor of the gargoyles at Notre Dame in Paris. The iconic raven. (Poe's big black bird seems to be everywhere in British Columbia.)

The *pièce de resistance* in the gallery is a cedar sculpture by Bill Reid. It is "The Raven and the First Man" based on a Haida Indian legend of flood survivors in a clam shell. A grim-faced, alert raven perches atop the shell with tiny men inside.

Another delight is the Science World, Vancouver's huge "golf ball." It's fun. Computer games. Puzzles. Demonstrations of scientific principles. Yet serious too. For instance, the world population is 6.2 billion and increasing every second.

Among the exhibits is a replica of the Sopwith Camel, the World War I fighter plane popularized by Snoopy. Also: the 1903 Kreiger car that ran on gas and electricity. Nearly a century later it may be the prototype of cars of the future.

Another don't-miss site is the Capilano suspension bridge in a rain forest north of Vancouver. It pitches and rolls like a ship in a storm-tossed sea. The bridge spans a narrow gorge 230 feet above the Capilano River. A huge boulder creates greenish white water.

Nearby is a "baby" Doug fir, just 350 years old with a life expectancy of 1,000 years. It will live well into the 27th century, making a visitor aware, not just of his mortality, but the shortness of human life.

One of the joys of travel is exotic people-watching. In the beautiful Queen Elizabeth Park, an Asiatic woman kneeled beside a low stone wall. With a large, gilt-edged, holy text in front of her, she raised her right hand as if blessing the wonders of Nature in the valley below. She chanted, praying with fervor. She may have been a Buddhist.

A ferry boat takes the tourist from Vancouver to Victoria, a veddy, veddy British city. It is essential to have high tea at the Empress. Oh, it's costly and snobby but the experience lasts a lifetime. Served are cucumber sandwiches, something this non-Brit had thought was an invention of Oscar Wilde in "The Importance of Being Earnest."

Victoria has two other wonderful places: the butterfly garden and the Butchart Gardens. The butterfly garden is full of beautiful creatures, some of which sit on your hand. The Butchart Gardens are world renowned. A profusion of flowers. Floral gardens. Sweet smell of blossoms.

Butchert Gardens has benches in quiet corners for contemplation and meditation. Life is really a series of such wonderful moments in the hurly-burly of living.

Sparks Tribune, June 20, 2002

Said, Riefenstahl, Plimpton requiem

The life of Edward Said makes you realize your own insignificance. He was a public intellectual, a Columbia University professor who was a prolific writer of important books and articles.

Above all, Said was a sane and eloquent voice for Palestine against the pro-Israel policy and hostility of the United States. He was a proud Palestinian exile who constantly pointed out that the pro-Israel media in America rarely tell of the injustices and cruelties of Israel.

Writer Alexander Cockburn extolled him as "the greatest Arab of his generation" with a "mighty and passionate heart."

Said, who died recently, saw the reality of Israel: a Western colony planted on Arab soil. He rightly lamented "the irreversible conquest of Palestinian land and society." He rightly expressed anger at the terrible wrongs of Israel: occupation of Arab lands, constant building of settlements in the West Bank and erection of an extensive barrier to them.

Said was "a critic of Western imperialism and a champion of Palestinian liberation," as The Nation noted.

Cockburn wrote something else true in this Dark Age of Bush, something that inspirits comrades of the Left: "We march through life buoyed by those comrades-in-arms we know to be marching with us, under the same banners, flying the same colors, sustained by the same hopes and convictions."

JoAnn Wypijewski, for many years Said's editor at The Nation, also made a true observation: "I've always thought that whatever else one might say about a person, if his children like him—not just love but like—he enters some superior category of esteem." Said's kids *liked* him.

•

On first seeing "Triumph of the Will," a 1934 documentary of a Nazi rally in Nuremberg, a violent anti-fascist is momentarily tempted to give the Nazi salute and cry, "Sieg Heil!" No wonder movie critic Pauline Kael called the director, Leni Riefenstahl, the greatest documentary filmmaker of all time.

Riefenstahl directed "Olympiad," a two-part documentary of the 1936 Berlin Olympics, which Kael called "a great lyric spectacle."

"She selected shots for their beauty rather than for a documentary record," Kael wrote. "After eighteen months of editing, she emerged with more than three hours of dazzling quality—films that move one kinesthetically in response to physical tension and psychologically in reponse to the anguish and strain of men and women desperately competing for a place in history...

"She knew beauty when she saw it: in the throbbing veins of Jesse Owens' forehead; in the lean Japanese swimmers; in the divers soaring in flight so continuous that they have no nationality."

The New York Times, in a recent obituary of the 101-year-old Riefenstahl, wrote that her Olympics documentary footage "included such innovative techniques as moving cameras, including one on a tiny elevator attached to a flagpole behind the speaker's lecturn that provided sweeping panoramic views; the use of telephoto lenses to create a foreshortening effect; frequent closeups of wide-eyed party faithful; and heroic poses of Hitler shot from well below eye level...

"To capture the drama of the pole vault and long jump events, she had holes dug beside the sand pits where the athletes landed. In the high-diving event, which dominated the second part of the film, 'Festival of Beauty,' she used four cameras, including one under water to capture the movement of divers from all angles."

Riefenstahl will forever be tainted as a propagandist for Hitler. But we must judge the *works* of artists, writers, composers, filmmakers–not their lives. Riefenstahl was a film genius.

●

In reality, Mitty is a henpecked husband and a bumbler in "The Secret Life of Walter Mitty," a great American short story written by James Thurber in 1939.

Ah, but in fantasy, Mitty is a famous surgeon, an heroic pilot of a Navy hydroplane, a crack shot, a possessor of "a lovely, dark-haired girl" and a World War I captain who swills brandy and jauntily hums *"Auprès de ma blonde"* while under intense artillery fire.

George Plimpton lived such fantasies for overweight and undertalented sports nuts. Plimpton, who died recently, boxed with light heavyweight champion Archie Moore and played with the Boston Celtics, Boston Bruins and Detroit Lions.

He faced Pancho Gonzales across a tennis net and played a golf match with another sports great, Sam Snead. He pitched in the All-Star baseball game, played chess with the world champion and fought in a bullfight.

These fantasies-become-reality were published as books and magazine articles to the delight of Joe Fan everywhere.

Sparks Tribune, Oct. 24, 2003

Arts and Letters

'Alice' endures despite dispute

SAN FRANCISCO—Perhaps I am insufficiently Freudian or lack the pruriency to see the Lewis Carroll photographs of young girls as smut.

I do know that newspaper copy editors must have a dirty mind to catch *double entrendres*. Example from a Canadian newspaper: "Sex education delayed; teachers request training." Example from a Virginia newspaper: "Lay position proposed by bishop for women."

Nevertheless, I find Carroll's photos of prepubescent girls anything but child pornography. The girls are not nymphets. They show "the spiritual beauty of the child." They show girls in serious, intense, sad-eyed, dreamy, pensive poses. They show the Victorian era's cult of the child, the belief in the innocence of children.

Carroll did take nude photos of girls (not displayed here) but only a pedophile would find them erotic. Young girls were Carroll's obsession. He loved them. But he did not molest them. They adored him.

(The Carroll photos are on display at the San Francisco Museum of Modern Art through Nov. 10.)

Carroll's favorite subject was Alice Liddell, daughter of Henry Liddell, Carroll's math dean at Oxford. Alice was the original audience for "Alice in Wonderland" and "Through the Looking Glass." Those classics may be the most widely read children's books in the world. They have been translated into more than 70 languages.

I recall reading "Alice" to my children. Periodically they would ask after my laughter: "What's so funny, daddy?" On one level they are kids' books. But on another they are humorous, satirical thrusts at the foibles and follies of adults.

The best photo in the exhibit is Alice as "The Beggar Maid" inspired by a Tennyson poem. She is dressed in rags. Her right hand is cupped to receive alms. Her shoulders are bare. It was just one of the many theaterical poses Carroll loved.

Just as beauty is in the eye of the beholder, so eroticism is in the eye of the onlooker. The photo is by no means erotic although some critics have suggested it is. To me, she is a sad-eyed waif.

Martin Gardner, who edited and wrote the introduction to "The Annotated Alice," called "Alice's Adventures in Wonderland" and "Through the Looking Glass" incomparable jests. In short, it is the Alice books that matter, not Carroll's obsession with young girls. The two books forever enrich literature, "a glorious artistic treasure."

'Eternal Egypt'

"Eternal Egypt," a collection of art and statuary from the British Museum, is not "worth a detour."

One reason is that the objects are familiar from numerous exhibits and pictures over the decades. Another is that the primitive religious rituals strike the modern viewer as absurd. But, then, you might say the same thing about symbols, rituals and incantations of religionists today.

(The exhibit is at the Palace of Legion of Honor through Nov. 11.)

Religion and art were entwined in ancient Egypt. Scholars have long observed that the life of ancient Egyptians was a long journey toward death.

The exhibit, the work of artisans spanning 30 centuries, really comes to life with the marvelous "Panel Portrait of a Woman." It was painted in color on limestone about 165 A.D. during the Roman occupation. The woman, a dark-eyed beauty, is wearing Greco-Roman dress.

Baseball by the Bay

Baseball fans who haven't been to the Giants' new stadium must do so at once. It has the inevitable corporate sponsor so this anti-corporatist will not print the name. But it's a wonderful place to watch the great game of baseball.

You gaze over the right and centerfield horizon to see the bay. The scoreboard gives you a wealth of information. Small scoreboards give you the mph of each pitch.

A big screen shows a replay of key plays. The same "window" gives useful information about the players. The area behind the stands is ringed with kids' games, miniature ball fields, restaurants and food booths.

The old knothole gang has been updated. You can stand and watch the game free. You go to the men's room and hear play-by-play. The corridors are loaded with TVs showing the game.

Oh, the concession stand prices are outrageous. A beer and a hotdog cost $11. Nevertheless, the park is a far cry from the ancestors of the Giants I saw play decades ago at the Polo Grounds in New York.

Sparks Tribune, Sept. 5, 2002

Wanted: UNR graduation speakers

It's time for the University of Nevada, Reno to scrap its terribly boring, terribly long graduation ceremonies.

When the school was much smaller and more bucolic, it was a nice touch to have each graduate shake hands with the university president and then walk across the stage. Grads get two seconds of fame, far less than Andy Warhol envisaged.

What should replace this dreary custom is a speaker of national prominence. Not the soporific types uttering platitudes. Needed are speakers of some renown who can deliver their message in 15 minutes.

Even if the speech is dull, it cannot be as boring as watching phalanx after phalanx of black-garbed graduates walking across the stage.

Sure, all the grads care about is getting out of college as fast as they can. But they would listen to someone with something to say. And even if they don't remember a word the speaker said, they will always be able to say that so-and-so spoke at their college commencement.

Moreover, the speaker might say something true, something astonishing—perhaps something inspiring.

This suggestion is prompted by a speech playwright Tony Kushner gave at the Vassar College commencement in May.

Kushner started with a paradox: "When you don't vote, you vote." To abstain is, in effect, to vote—to sustain the status quo. Republicans vote far more than Democrats because they know what is at stake in politics.

"When you accept the loony logic of some on the Left that there is no political value in supporting the lesser of two evils, you open the door to the greater evil," Kushner said.

The greater evil is George W. Bush. As Kushner puts it, it is evil to:

"Abolish the Clean Air Act and the Kyoto accords and refuse to participate in the World Court or the ban on landmines. Evil is happily refusing funds to American clinics overseas that counsel abortion and evil is happily drilling for oil in Alaska. Evil is happily pinching pennies while 40 million people worldwide suffer and perish from AIDS."

Then Kushner segues into Emerson. "You should all read Emerson, all the time," he told the Vassar grads.

He harks back to the address Emerson gave to the graduating class of the Harvard divinity school in 1838. Kushner's refrain line to the Vassar grads is to speak the truth just as Emerson told the Harvard grads that the preacher's task was "to convert life into truth."

Doubtless Kusher and Emerson are too erudite for UNR grads. But life is much more than just getting a job. It is a lifetime of learning, reading, experiencing—and seeking the truth.

Emerson (1803-1882) gave another lecture, "The American Scholar," that was even more celebrated than his Harvard talk. It was an oration before the Phi Beta Kappa Society in Cambridge, Mass., in 1837.

In it Emerson spoke of "the love of letters." He extolled the scholar, "the delegated intellect…Man Thinking." (Thinking is precisely what most people don't want to do, including college graduates.)

Just as the character of people can be judged by the books they have in their home, so Emerson could divine much from their speech. "I learn immediately from any speaker how much he has already lived through the poverty or splendor of his speech," Emerson told the Phi Betas.

Emerson, probably the most famous essayist in American history, wrote his best essay in "Self-Reliance." It crackles with such lines as these:

"Whoso would be a man must be a nonconformist…(But) for nonconformity the world whips you with its displeasure...Nothing is at last sacred but the integrity of our own mind...To be great is to be misunderstood...every stoic was a stoic but in Christendom where is the Christian?"

Like his Concord, Mass., friend Thoreau, Emerson reverenced nature. In an essay on history, Emerson wrote: "The man who has seen the rising moon break out of the clouds at midnight has been present like an archangel at the creation of light and of the world."

Emerson's judgment sometimes was faulty. He was too optimistic. He put too much reliance on what he called the "oversoul" (God) rather than the self-reliance he urged.

And he badly misjudged Thoreau, lamenting that Thoreau lacked ambition. "Wanting this, instead of engineering for all America, he was the captain of a huckleberry party," Emerson wrote.

He was wrong. The country could use many more such captains of berry-picking parties.

In any case, a speaker of stature would make UNR commencements more stimulating and more memorable.

Sparks Tribune, Oct. 3, 2002

Art makes desert bloom

LAS VEGAS—This is not the kind of city that sophisticated people choose to live in. It squats in the desert, its sole *raison d'être* a worldwide gambling mecca.

It is too glitzy and too crowded with tourists. It lacks culture and packs a superabundance of things that do not matter. It is jammed with people who, if they read any newspaper at all, read the lightweight USA Today. It exemplifies what's wrong with America.

Sure, Las Vegas has many fine people like Mike Green, history professor at the Community College of Southern Nevada, and Geoff Schumacher, editor of the Mercury. But for the most part the city is a vast wasteland as was once famously said of TV.

Las Vegas is geographically and metaphorically a desert. But one thing makes the desert bloom: its wonderful art.

First and foremost is The Wynn Collection on the Strip. I have never seen so much great art packed in so small a place—not in the old Courtauld of London, not in the Frick of New York. The Wynn exhibit of 14 paintings is shown in a single gallery about 12 yards wide and 25 yards long.

Tears came to my eyes on seeing the works of famed artists in the most unlikely of places: "Sodom and Gomorrah."

The collection contains two masterpieces, van Gogh's "Peasant Woman Against a Background of Wheat" (1890), and Picasso's "Le Rêve" (The Dream) painted in 1932.

The van Gogh is luminous. The woman is wearing a yellow straw hat and a blue dress. Poppies dot the rich, green wheatfield. Its thick brush strokes are a van Gogh trademark. And the colors, always the colors.

The Picasso, worth about $50 million, is a mix of bright colors and eroticism. The woman tilts her head horizontally with a dreamy expression. Reds, greens, yellows abound. Next to the painting is a photograph taken by Man Ray in 1932. It shows a young Picasso: handsome, dark, virile and intensely serious.

Wynn, the billionaire casino tycoon, narrates the audio guide to the exhibit with proper solemnity. But his frequent outbursts of enthusiasm mark him as a true amateur. About the van Gogh, Wynn says:"The fluidity and the richness of the paint, the boldly executed brushwork and the vibrancy of the colors are exceptional—even for van Gogh."

Other artists exhibited include Monet and Manet, Pissarro and Gauguin, Cezanne and Modigliani. Then a delightful surprise: three panels of Wynn captured by Andy Warhol in 1983 with his trusty Polaroid. (Silkscreen ink and diamond dust on canvas.)

Libby Lumpkin, art professor at the University of Nevada-Las Vegas, says Wynn wanted to give Las Vegas "a new elegance and refinement." He certainly has.

Also lending elegance to Las Vegas is the Guggenheim Hermitage at the Venetian. Its "Masterpieces of Painting from Titian to Picasso" include art by Velásquez and Delacroix, Gainsborough and Reynolds, Monet and van Gogh and Durer and Rubens. Among moderns are works by Chagall, Rothko, Pollock, Lichtenstein and de Kooning.

The Titian stars Lucretia, shining with bright flesh color. Reynolds shows cupid untying a love knot on a coquettish woman with a come-hither look, her breasts bare, an arm coyly hiding half of her face.

As for the Picasso, the 1904 painting in gray shows a gaunt woman ironing. She presses down on the iron as if pushed by an oppressor. Her head tilts, her left eye has a dark circle of despair.

The desert also blooms at the Bellagio Gallery of Fine Art with an exhibition of celebrity portraits by Andy Warhol. (Warhol is famed for his Campbell's soup series and for remarking: "In the future everyone will be world famous for 15 minutes." He also remarked sagely: "Buying is much more American than thinking.")

Artists carve out their own niche, create their own style. Warhol's niche was "celebrity wallpaper." The exhibit includes many of his blurry, colored pictures of celebrities: Marilyn (Monroe), Liz (Taylor), Jackie (Kennedy), Mick (Jagger) and Mickey (Mouse).

One fine example of Warhol pop-art is a pair of portraits of Alfred Hitchcock with sketch lines inside his celebrated profile. Another outstanding display is that of Jewish giants of the 20th century including Marx and Freud, a pensive Sarah Bernhardt and a thoughtful Louis Brandeis, Supreme Court justice who was a leading Zionist.

Art, like music, is a universal language. It speaks magnificently amid the kitsch of Las Vegas.

Sparks Tribune, April 3, 2003

Reflections on artists

Peter Schjeldahl, The New Yorker art critic, knows one thousand times more about art than I ever will. Yet one of his recent statements must be challenged. He writes that Velázquez is "almost certainly the greatest of painters."

That opinion is absurd. It reminds me of a friend who tells of writing an essay in a New Orleans high school. The teacher wrote on it: "Winifred. This is a sweeping statement." (Sweeping statement was underlined.) In other words, an overstatement, a gross exaggeration.

Schjeldahl also writes in the same article that Velázquez (1559-1660) exemplified in his painting a "fusion of truth and beauty."

Truth as the royal court painter in Spain? A painter whose first portrait of Philip II revealed him as the homely man he was? A painter whose portraits of Philip grew more and more circumspect and less and less truthful? A painter whose last portraits of him reeked of sycophancy?

At least the Time-Life book (1975) is more limited in its sweeping statements. It calls Velázquez "the greatest of *Spanish* painters." (My italics.)

Ok. Velázquez is marvelous. But he was not even the greatest Spanish painter. Goya was. Goya, with his dark vision, filled so many canvases with his black view of the human condition. Goya was far closer to the truth than Velázquez.

Either in your home library or in a public library, take a look again at Van Gogh's "The Potato Eaters." It can be argued that *this* is the greatest painting. Yes, it may be crude. It does not have the elegance of Velázquez. Indeed, thousands of paintings might be purer and smoother.

But "The Potato Eaters" is a *cri de coeur* for socialism, for humanity. Surely that is greater than all the artistry of Velázquez, all his pictures of royalty and nobility.

"The Potato Eaters" reminds you of the Edwin Markham poem, "The Man with the Hoe":

"Bowed by the weight of centuries he leans / Upon his hoe and gazes on the ground, / The emptiness of ages in his face, / And on his back the burden of the world...

"Stolid and stunned, a brother to the ox? /...Slave of the wheel of labor...Through this dread shape humanity betrayed, / Plundered, profaned and disinherited."

"The Potato Eaters" (1885) is painted in dark, earth tones. It shows the grim, hard life of the Dutch peasants. They are eating in a crude room which has been described as humble-looking as a stable. They poke at boiled potatoes. Loneliness shows on their gnarled, resigned faces.

Although Van Gogh's canvases often bedazzle with color, his sketches and drawings often bear "the eternal note of sadness."

A Sparks friend, Bill Hall, writes: "I saw a Van Gogh drawing (pen, ink, pencil) of a nude woman hunched over, breasts hanging, in an art book. It was titled 'Sorrow.' It was the saddest rendering of human sorrow I have ever seen."

Low fat food tasteless

Grocery shelves are full of low-fat or no-fat items. All such products might be good for the waistline but terrible for the tastebuds. Better to take in a few more calories rather than eat such flat food.

Picking up pennies

Am I the only one who still picks up pennies left on the street? Maybe it is a habit connected with an impoverished boyhood. (Sob, sob.) I am *only* five cents richer each week because of such thriftiness. But at least I can use them for giving exact change.

But I wonder why mints still produce pennies? They cost the government much more to make than they are worth. The British long go abandoned the farthing, the French the centime.

'Have a nice day'

It began as a polite phrase used by clerks in stores: "Have a nice day." Now nearly everyone uses it.

It's harmless expression. People who use it mean well. But it is treacly and awfully frayed. Perhaps that's why I love the contrarian spirit of this bumper sticker: "I'll have any damn kind of day I please."

Renouncing thinking

Someone—perhaps it was Albert Schweitzer—has characterized American society as one that renounces thinking. No further evidence of that truth need be adduced than the ignorant warmonger placed in the White House by vote-stealing Florida officials and five ideologues on the Supreme Court.

Sparks Tribune, Jan. 2, 2003

Touch of class in Reno

Reno has entered the major leagues of art houses with its marvelous new Nevada Museum of Art. So far, exhibitions are big league too.

The museum has had two shows this summer which could be called blockbusters in "the biggest little city in the world." One is "Diego Rivera and 20th century Mexican Art," the other "Edward Hopper: the Paris Years."

Impressive. Truckee Meadows denizens think so too. One Friday morning in late June, a visitor stood in line for 12 minutes to get into the Rivera show. Lines for a Reno art exhibit once were unheard of. Earlier in June, 11,000 turned out for the grand opening. Total attendees for the first month: 40,000.

The building at 160 W. Liberty St. is an imposing work of art itself, looking like a huge, gray ship surrounded by sculpture at "the water level."

The NMA, designed by architect Will Bruder, has four floors. The ground floor houses a 180-seat theater, a café and a store. The second floor has a library, galleries and a wonderful "discovery center" with easels, drawing paper and drawing pencils where young and old can pretend they are artists.

The third floor has more galleries. The open-topped fourth floor is a jewel. It holds a sculpture court, provides cityscapes and views of the hills surrounding Reno. In a stroke of architectural genius, the roof top offers a view of distant Mount Rose (10,778 feet).

In the atrium, a semi-circular black staircase leads to the ceiling. Bruder describes it: "We wound the staircase up to the sky and it literally does go up to the sky. It's a slender penetration like a crevase up a canyon. It draws you up." Bruder also extols the skylights. They "manipulate the light as it changes through the day and seasons, becoming like weaving a beautiful quilt."

In the Mexican art exhibit, Frida Kahlo's paintings are fraught with the physical and psychological pain she suffered from a streetcar accident, two troubled marriages with the faithless Diego Rivera, and a suicide attempt. (The Kahlo exhibit has left Reno but the Rivera and Hopper shows continue through Sept. 21.)

Surrealist and dadaist Andre Breton claimed Kahlo as "one of us" but Kahlo denied it. "I paint my own reality," she answered. She does indeed let all her wounds and angst fill her canvases. Which is why this viewer is not bowled over by her work. Still, it is great to be able to see her paintings in Reno.

Rivera is far better known as a muralist. His murals are revolutionary, which led to one of the great tragedies of art history. His mural in Rockefeller Center in New York City was destroyed because it had a portrait of Lenin.

In the Reno exhibit, two well-known Rivera paintings are exhibited. One is "Calla Lily Vendor." The sombrero of the vendor and the flowers hide his face. Two girls kneel in front of the monumental flower "portrait." The other is a 1943 portrait of Natasha Gelman in a Hollywood glamour pose. She is wearing a white dress opening at the legs to make her look like a calla lily. (The traveling Mexican art exhibit is from the Jacques and Natasha Gelman Collection.)

The Hopper exhibit, from the first decade of the 20th century, obviously doesn't include the famous "Nighthawks." Nor does it have the "New York Movie," a portrait of loneliness that Hopper canvases often portray. The blonde usher leans against a wall, depressed, sad-faced in a boring, dead-end job.

The Hopper show, traveling to Reno through the courtesy of the Whitney Museum of Modern Art in New York, disappoints. It's an exhibit of paintings from Hopper's immature years. Some of the paintings are amateurish. Two views of Notre Dame cathedral might have been painted by any beginner. Still, it is good to see the works of an American "star" in Reno.

The best of the show: "Le Bistro or the Wine Shop" (1909) with a white bridge, four populars bending in the breeze and two women drinking wine at an outside table.

In front of the art gallery is a sculpture in two-foot tall pink marble blocks. It reads: "Inhale, exhale." Good advice. It's like the marvelous advice of a celebrated golfer of yesteryear, Walter Haig: "Smell the flowers along the way."

The NMA brings a touch of class to a city saturated with uncouth gambling.

Sparks Tribune, July 24, 2003

Sad tale of Allende overthrow

"Amigas" is a closet drama, a play better read than staged. But the words of the two-character, two-act play are worth listening to. They offer a lament for a lost homeland, a cry for social justice and serious talk leavened with humor.

Jeanmarie Simpson and Martina Young, stalwarts of the Nevada Shakespeare Co., present the trials and triumphs of two friends from their days in Chile, Emma Sepulveda and Marjorie Agosin. Young plays Emma, Simpson is Marjorie.

"Amigas" had its world premiere July 17 at the new Nevada Museum of Art in Reno before an audience of about 100. The play, written by Simpson and Young, is based on an exchange of letters between Sepulveda and Agostin published in their book, "Amigas: Letters of Friendship and Exile." Sepulveda is Spanish professor at the University of Nevada, Reno. Agosin teaches at Wellesley in Massachusetts.

The central trauma for Emma and Marjorie is the coup toppling Allende, socialist president of Chile, by Pinochet, human rights abuser *extraordinaire*. Emma tells of her agony when Allende is overthrown Sept. 11, 1973—the first 9/11 tragedy.

She calls Allende a great man who shook her hand while he was campaigning at her university in Santiago.

"Allende said that to find our true destiny on the global stage, we have to educate our youth, liberate the working class and nationalize Chile's resources," Emma says. "He spoke of the injustices in the countryside, that not only does the laborer work for beggarly wages but that women and children work without earning a cent."

Emma naively notes that she could not believe the CIA "would meddle in the internal affairs of another country." Little did she know how far capitalism spreads its ugly tentacles, little did she know of U.S. economic imperialism and gunboat diplomacy in Latin America, and little did she know that the United States loudly proclaims its love for democracy—but not if democracy means electing socialists.

But she and Marjorie did know they must flee Chile.

Emma is a Catholic, Marjorie a Jew. Emma is from aristocratic society, Marjorie middle class but "an intellectual household." Marjorie says: "It would be unthinkable to say that one is a pure Jew but isn't an intellectual."

Emma tells of her anguish over an abusive father, the death of two brothers, and a mother's suffering from a brutal, womanizing husband. "How my father always hit her…how he punched me as if I were a man," she says.

Years later Emma learns sadly that in America, too, "where there is so much it all seems to be destined for the few." She runs—and loses—in a race for the state Senate in 1994, learning that "elections belong to whoever amasses the most money (while) the businesses buy the candidates at a good price."

Marjorie is always the poet. In Chile, she rhapsodizes: "I love feeling the night arrive, very dense, the nighttime next to the sea, the beautiful night, the golden night." She prefers "to spend entire nights gazing at the stars with an imaginary telescope or writing poems by candlelight and the scent of lavender."

She extols Chile's two greatest poets, Gabriela Mistral and Pablo Neruda. Mistral: the first woman poet to win the Nobel Prize for literature and first Latin American so honored (1945). Neruda: militant communist, exilist and Nobelist (1971).

Marjorie is not nearly as political as Emma. Whenever Emma talks of Allende, Marjorie changes the subject. It's a false note in a serious work. The presentation is also marred by instrusive background music—jazz, guitar, Latino pop tunes—that "steps on" the dialogue. Young sometimes drops her voice, sometimes speaks too fast. But Simpson is always winning and convincing.

A fascinating byplay in the drama are *arpillera,* colorful, tapestries woven by Chilean women to protest the murders, executions, political prisoners, tortures and disappearances. (The Pinochet death toll: 10,000.) The embroidered cloth rectangles are "message" montages— names of the missing (*desaparecidos*) with the recurring question: "doñde estan?" ("Where are they?")

Periodically during the play, the *arpilleras* are hung *behind* the black curtain and only shown at the end. It would have been far preferable for director Cameron Crain to have had them hung out front during the play.

The end of the performance was greeted by a standing ovation it did not merit. American audiences are too prone to give standing Os, stripping the gesture of all significance.

Sparks Tribune, Aug. 1, 2003

Reflections on writing

One of the keenest observations ever made about the craft of writing was offered by naturalist Buffon in his admission speech to the French Academy in 1753: "The style is the man himself."

Hemingway, one of the great stylists in American literature, was punchy and terse. Another American writer, Faulkner, often wrote in a difficult, stream-of-consciousness style.

Their totally different styles reveal what Strunk and White in "The Elements of Style" calls their literary fingerprints: "All writers, by the way they use the language, reveal something of their spirits, their habits, their capacities and their biases."

The Strunk-White book is fewer than 100 pages packed in a small paperback. But in boxing parlance, it is pound for pound the best book on writing ever written. It should be read once a year by all writers. But the revisers should shed archaisms still in the fourth edition of the book, which was first published by Professor Strunk nearly 100 years ago.

For instance, Strunk-White insists on a comma in a series: red, white, and blue. The second comma is unnecessary. A comma means a pause. The reader does not pause after white.

S-W insists on a placing a comma before a conjunction introducing an independent clause as in: "the Cubans doubtless knew it, because they..." The comma is unnecessary. Readers do not pause before because. S-W insists on Burns's poetry. The second s is unnecessary.

S-W urges use of semi-colons in constructions like these: "Mary Shelley's works are entertaining; they are full of engaging ideas." The modern way: "Mary Shelley's works are entertaining. They are full of..." Semi-colons are obsolete except in a series. (Sally Smith, president; Tim Jones, vice president; and Sue Foster, secretary.)

Other sound advice on writing. Thoreau: "You must work very long to write short sentences." Voltaire: "the adjective is the enemy of the noun." Orwell too in his 1946 essay on "Politics and the English Language":

• "Never use a metaphor, simile or other figure of speech that you are used to seeing in print." (cliché)

• "Never use a long word where a short one will do." (pedantry)

• "If it is possible to cut a word out, always cut it out." (conciseness)

• "Never use the passive where you can use the active." (impact)

Ben Franklin, member of an intellectual club in colonial Philadelphia, the Junto, had to write an essay once every three months. In one essay, Franklin asked: what qualities should good writing have? His answer: "It should be smooth, clear and short." Sound advice 250 years later.

Contrast the Franklin way with the abominable, abstract and meaningless prose so often associated with academics. Example:

"If, for a while, the ruse of desire is calculable for the uses of discipline soon the repetition of guilt, justification, pseudo-scientific theories, superstitition, spurious authorities and classifications can be seen as the desperate effort to 'normalize' formally..."

There is still more to that sentence. But why go on? The point is clear: the writer has succeeded in keeping his wisdom to himself. Nor is that thicket of prose made up. The writer is Homi Bhabha, star of the Afro-American studies department at Harvard.

Oh, and please: don't ask your computer to evaluate your writing. Examples of computerese feedback: "This does not seem to be a complete sentence." (Fragments go back at least as far as Dickens in "Bleak House.")

Or: "It is better not to begin sentences with 'and' and 'but.' " Nonsense. A friend told me that he went to a parochial school where a nun told him: "Never began a sentence with and—unless you have a college education." Start with a conjunction with or without a college degree.

In England the Apostrophe Protection Society is campaigning to have apostrophes put where they belong— and eliminated where they don't. Some targets: "menu's," "ladies fashions" and "mans" barbershop. (Menus doesn't take an apostrophe and it should be ladies' and man's.)

Why the apostrophe in 1960's? (New York Times usage) It is not possessive. Why the apostrophe in CD's? It is not possessive.

So I sympathize with the society as trivial a matter as it may seem. It is hell going through life with a proofreader's mentality as I have for 50 years as a writer and editor. (I chafed when I saw a message outside a Reno casino. It read: "Les Folie's de Paris." How that apostrophe got there I leave to the gods presiding over the abuse of the language.)

In any case, all writers have a style. And by that style ye shall know them—favorably or unfavorably.

Sparks Tribune, Nov. 28, 2002

141

On editing and Christianity

Everyone who writes, whether for a church bulletin, a newspaper or a novel, needs an editor, a second pair of eyes to vet what is written.

Rereading Somerset Maugham's "Moon and Sixpence" recently, I found myself taking out such lame modifiers as "rathers" and "somewhats." I read "one another" rather than the correct "each other." Scribbling in my paperback, I crossed out "not infrequently" and made it "frequently." I saw a "which" that should have been "that."

Maugham was a good writer. Alas, I am just a good editor. I'd trade being a good writer for a good editor any time.

An ad in a recent New Yorker tells how Teddy Roosevelt wrote 35 books on topics ranging from naval history to wildlife. Then: "And, of course, he enjoyed a fulfilling life with his wife and children." Why of course? Of course is one of the most overused expressions in writing. It's particularly galling when it is not self-evident as in the TR "of course."

One of the things that annoys this editor is when a writer—either in a newspaper story or a book—fails to give the "whys" of a something. (Some reporters are insulted if their sacred copy is edited or questions are asked of them.) For instance, in "Goodbye to All That," Robert Graves writes that the poet Swinburne was "a public menace." Why? Graves writes that Christ was not "the perfect man." Why?

He writes that he "could not stand life at Charterhouse (school)." Why? Graves writes: "I found serious conversation with my parents all but impossible." Why? He writes of "Freud's more idiosyncratic theses." Such as?

Graves writes that poet Sassoon "began to write the terrifying sequence of poems." What poems? Why terrifying? Graves writes that his wife was disgusted with the wedding service. Why?

Such statements are worthless. Without answers to the whys and examples of the "such ases," readers cannot judge the validity of an author's statements.

●

Point of view is everything. I wrote a column years ago about the marvels of nature, concluding with a rhapsodic vision of being unable to set a price on the sight of a flock of geese flying overhead at sunset. But, ah, Canadian geese become less marvelous when you see their droppings staining the walkways in Reno's Rancho San Rafael park.

●

As a university journalism teacher for decades, I have been denouncing grade inflation, urging tougher grading standards. It is a lost cause. But Major League Baseball doesn't have standards either.

The San Francisco Giants were playing the Florida Marlins about a year ago. The score was 1-1 in the ninth inning. Two were out but the Giants had a runner on first base. A batter hit a drive to the left of the center fielder. After a hard run, he caught the ball momentarily—and then dropped it. The runner scored, the Giants won, 2-1.

Point: the batter was credited with a runs-batted-in two-base hit. But it should have been scored as an error. The fielder clearly should have caught the ball.

I thought of the time five decades ago I kept the official score of American Legion baseball games in Franklin, Pa. Hitters complained when I ruled errors on what they thought were hits. Standards. They must prevail in baseball and academia no matter the complaints of athletes and students.

●

I remember as a boy how the prices of candy bars would go up while packages shrunk. I did not realize at the time that that was the Grand Old Capitalist Way. Well, it's still the GOCW.

143

Frito-Lay today is putting fewer chips in bags of Fritos and Chee-tos. ChapStick tubes are smaller, prices higher.

Andy Rooney, essayist on CBS's "60 Minutes," notes the same phenomenon with cans of coffee. Cans still come in one-pound size but contain just 11 ounces of coffee. Coffee prices, meanwhile, go up and up.

Many consumers are unaware of the fraud. (Industry insiders mask the deception with euphemism: the weighout.)

•

Columnist Molly Ivins wrote in praise of a wonderful Texas congressman, Bob Eckhardt, who had just died. In one moving paragraph, she wrote:

"At least 60 years ago someone said to his mother, 'Mrs. Eckhardt, your son is just a little too cozy with the nigras, don't you think?" She replied sweetly: 'Oh, I'm afraid that's my fault. I raised him to be a Christian.' "

Sparks Tribune, Aug. 14, 2003

'Art elevates the soul'

SAN FRANCISCO—The fantasy world of Marc Chagall grows on you. Lovers flying over villages. People lying on the snow in front of houses for no apparent reason. Roosters in unexpected places and positions. And fiddlers on rooftops.

This Chagall fantasyland at the San Francisco Museum of Modern Art is a stunning exhibit, worth a special visit for Truckee Meadows art lovers. (Showing through Nov. 4.) Many of the 140 paintings show the absolute *joie de vivre* of Chagall: images of dancers, singers, acrobats and actors.

As Chagall (1887-1985) said: "Art elevates the soul of humanity."

He also has said he prays when he paints. This is evident in "The Apparition." The canvas is divided by colors from the upper left to the lower right. The artist sits at his easel on the left, swathed in grays and blacks. The upper right triangle is bluish, surrounding a hovering angel.

Kenneth Baker, art critic for the San Francisco Chronicle, writes: "In it, an angelic muse descends to inspire Chagall in his studio with a great churning of Cubo-Futuristic ideas."

The long love affair of Chagall and his beloved Bella is evident on many of the canvases, holding hands, kissing, flying together. One, "Bella with Carnation," is a traditional portrait but a fine one. It shows Bella as a Hamletesque figure with black tunic, white color and long black hair. She looks wise, thoughtful, philosophic and theatrical.

•

Do you want to own your own Chagall? You can buy a nice Chagall lithograph, "Candlestick," with green and blue paint predominating, for $2,500 at the Christopher-Clark Fine Art gallery at 377 Geary St.

Yes, $2,500 is a lot of money for most people, especially those struggling to pay the rent let alone put original art on the wall. But it could be doable for some.

On the contrary, one lovely Chagall at the gallery, "Adam and Eve and the Forbidden Fruit," sells for $19,800—too rich for the blood of most people who President Bush hasn't shed his blessings on with tax cuts. Still, it's a lovely work with both figures nude.

The gallery is featuring the art of La Belle Epoque with many original Toulouse-Lautrec lithos. The high end for a Lautrec is $169,850—far too pricey for all but the very rich. But on the lower end is an affordable ($1,950) TL sheet-music cover.

The gallery has much else worth looking at: original Picassos, Renoirs, Tissots, Bonnards and Müchas (whose posters of Sarah Bernhardt advertise plays and products.) Moreover, you can look at such good art gratis.

•

"Chicago" has been around for years now, most recently in movie houses. But it is a first-rate musical as anyone attending the revival at Golden Gate Theatre will attest.

It's jazzy, lively, full of verve. The joy of living is palpable in the dancing, singing and acting. From the opening number, "All That Jazz," the musical wins the affection of even the sourest pusses.

Newspaper people will particularly enjoy the press scenes with their echoes of "The Front Page," a 1928 play by Ben Hecht and Charles MacArthur. Lawyers and people who know legal gambits will revel in the satiric razzle-dazzle defense for murderers. (The facts be damned.)

A sardonic tone pervades the production, celebrating murder, justice unserved and a cynical number about the United States being the greatest country in the world. (It would never get by the former Hays and Breen codes that hobbled movies for decades.)

One of the pleasures of a visit to San Francisco, the best city in America, is Grace Cathedral, a concrete Episcopal monument modeled on the great cathedrals of Europe.

Out front are the bronze "doors of paradise," copies of the Ghiberti (1378-1455) masterpiece on the doors of the Baptistry in Florence. (One of the panels shows Noah lying drunk under a barrel of wine. [Genesis 9:21])

Inside is the Chapel of Grace. Its design and stained class were inspired by Sainte Chapelle in Paris with its narrow, lengthy glass. The floor tapestry inside the entrance to the cathedral, the labyrinth, is based on the medieval pavement design in the Chartres Cathedral. In a wonderful tradition at Grace, visitors take their shoes off to walk the maze-like path for spiritual uplift.

Leave the last word to cathedral dean Alan Jones: "A cathedral is for pilgrims of the spirit."

Sparks Tribune, Aug. 21, 2003

King James Bible still shines

The two greatest literary triumphs of the Elizabethan Age were Shakespeare and the King James Bible.

Shakespeare is incomparable now and forever despite the fact that some lit majors in college aren't required to take him. The King James Bible is what James Wood, writing in The New Yorker earlier this year, called "a great music."

The KJB has simplicity, grace and eloquence. It is both a religious and a literary classic. It is what author Alister McGrath calls "perhaps the greatest contribution to the spiritual ennobling of the human race."

Shakespeare's most magnificent output coincides with the creation of the KJB from 1604 to 1611. Normally works produced by committee are bad. But not the KJB. It was produced by a scholarly committee—six companies of nine men each—to produce what has been called the "noblest monument of English prose."

The committee included such men as John Bois, who wrote Hebrew at 6 and entered Cambridge at 14. Another committee member, Miles Smith, should be honored for one statement alone: he was "covetous of nothing but books."

The Italians have a wonderful saying: to translate is to betray (*traduttore traditore*). Translation is an art. Translators can get the meanings right but so often they miss the nuance, the spirit.

For example, it is extremely difficult to translate Shakespeare. But the André Gide translation of "Hamlet" (1946) captures both the words and the spirit. "Shakespeare is not a 'thinker,' " Gide writes. "He is a poet. And his thought hardly matters without the wings that carry him to empyrean heights."

The translators of the Hebrew and Greek biblical texts caught the words and "music." But they did not have to work *ab ovo*. Sixty percent of the KJB is based on Bible translations of men like William Tyndale and Miles Cloverdale. As the great physicist Isaac Newton said: "If I have seen farther it is by standing on the shoulders of giants."

Tyndale translations can be found in the KJB such as: "The powers that be" (Romans 13:1), "the salt of the earth" (Matthew 5:13) and "a law unto themselves" (Romans 2:14).

New translations of the Bible seem to come out yearly. But not one is worth the King James Version. Oh, the new versions are more modern and more easily understood in some passages. But they lack the beauty, the poetry and the literary qualities of the KJB.

Take the story of the nativity in Luke. Modern versions have Joseph going to Bethlehem with Mary "who was expecting a child" or is "pregnant." Compare that mundaneness with the KJB: Mary was "great with child."

Or try Matthew 4:19 in a politically correct modern version: "Follow me and I will make you fish for people." Now look at KJB: "Follow me and I will make you fishers of men." The first is flat. The KJB version is literature. Modern version of Matthew 17:5: "This is my son, the beloved; he enjoys my favor." The KJB is so much better: "This is my beloved son, in whom I am well pleased."

Ruth says in the KJB: "Whither thou goest, I will go; and where thou lodgest, I will lodge." The Living Bible version is absurd: "Don't make me leave you for I want to go wherever you go." Cain, asked where his brother Abel is, replies memorably: "Am I my brother's keeper?" The Living Bible renders it pallid and prosey: "Am I supposed to keep track of him wherever he goes?"

Typographical errors have been the bane of Bible publication for centuries. Some have been howlers as the so-called Wicked Bible of 1632 printed in London. The *not* was dropped from the seventh commandment to read: "Thou shalt commit adultery."

Then there was the Placemakers' Bible of 1562, the second edition of the Geneva Bible, which rendered Matthew 5:9: "Blessed are the placemakers" instead of the peacemakers. The Unrighteous Bible printed in Cambridge in 1653 had the unrighteous inheriting the earth.

As Oscar Wilde quipped: "A poet can survive anything except a misprint." The Bible obviously has survived misprints. And it will last forever in the King James Version even if fewer and fewer religious denominations use it.

Macaulay put the case for the KJB succinctly: "The English Bible, a book which if everything else in our language should perish, would alone suffice to show the whole extent of its beauty and power."

No wonder Gideons International places the KJB in hotels, motels and hospitals worldwide.

Sparks Tribune, Sept. 11, 2003

Faith vs. reason

"A History of God" by Karen Armstrong is well worth reading for the theologically and intellectually inclined. Yes, many parts are abstruse and there are many *longueurs*. Moreover, the book is sometimes hard for nonbelievers to read, rejecting as they do the concept of a God.

Yet the history of religion and mankind's historic belief in gods and God are always worth pondering. So are the views of leading theologians and philosophers.

In the preface to her book (published 10 years ago), Armstrong offers opinions and raises questions that have troubled theologians and laymen for centuries. Such as:

• "It is inappropriate for people who call themselves Jews, Christians and Muslims to condone an inequitable social system."

• Some religious people tell Armstrong that God is "a product of the creative imagination" and that a few highly respected have told her that God does not exist.

• Science seems to have disposed "of the Creator God" and bibilical scholars have "proved that Jesus never claimed to be divine."

• "Christian fundamentalists seem to have little regard for the loving compassion of Christ."

• "How could a perfect and infinite God have created a finite world riddled with evil?"

Armstrong, a former nun, is a teacher, writer and religious commentor. She invites readers to debate with themselves the concepts of original sin, the doctrine of afterlife, the Trinity and the meaning of life.

She writes of the views of theological and philosophical giants:

• Maimonides (1135-1204), Talmudist and philosopher, who believed God was "incomprehensible and inaccessible to human reason," that he "remains ineffable and indescribable," beyond our intellects.

• Dun Scotus, ninth century Celtic philosopher, maintained that faith and reason were not mutually exclusive. And Aquinas in the 13th century called "excessive intellectualism damaging to the faith." It was Aquinias who cited among his "proofs" for the existence of God that of the Prime Mover and the arguments from design.

The sins in the name of religion are not ignored. Armstrong notes that even some 17th century Christians "were embarrassed by the cruelty of so much Christian history...fearful Crusades, inquisitions and persecutions in the name of God." Also: burnings at the stake of so-called heretics.

Armstrong quotes the 12th century abbot in France who "urged Crusaders to show their love of Christ by killing the infidels and driving them out of the Holy Land." The Catholic Church denounced Copernicus and Galileo for pointing out that the sun was the center of the universe.

Nor does she spare Martin Luther, so right about his indictment of indulgences and buying entrance into heaven. Armstrong writes scathingly of him: rabid anti-Semite, misogynist, "convulsed with loathing and horror of sexuality," who believed that all rebellious peasants should be killed." Nor Calvin: he of the obnoxious doctrine that some were predestined to be saved but "the rest to eternal damnation."

Spinoza thought that "the rites and symbols of the faith could only help the masses who were incapable of scientific, rationale thought." Kant "dismissed many of the trappings of religion such as the dogmatic authority of the churches, prayer and ritual." Newton wanted to do away with all "the superstition and foolishness of religion."

The deists seen to get the better of the argument with their God of reason. But to me, even celebrated deists like

Voltaire and Paine suffered from a failure of intellect and a failure of nerve. Intellect would have told them that there is no God. The failure of nerve comes in refusal to disavow what "everybody believes.

The author concludes with the two strongest chapters: "The Death of God?" and "Does God Have a Future?" Great thinkers are invoked. Marx on religion: "the sigh of the oppressed creature...the *opium* of the people." And Feuerbach: "God was simply a human projection." (Marx was appalled by a God who condoned social injustice.)

Freud believed that "God is an illusion that mature men and women should lay aside."And Camus rightly argued that "a passionate and committed atheism can be more religious than a weary or inadequate theism."

Still, Armstrong provides much support for the belief in God, presenting the arguments of some of the great theologians of the 20th century: Altizer, Barth, Tillich and Buber.

It comes down to faith versus reason. For me, reason wins. But most people prefer Paul in Hebrews 11:1: "Now faith is the substance of things hoped for the evidence of things not seen."

Sparks Tribune, Sept. 18, 2003

Supreme Court

Supreme Court: ever rightward

5-4, 5-4, 5-4, 5-4, 5-4, 5-4, 5-4.

It's sickening. The five reactionaries on the Supreme Court continue to make outrageous law of the land. Nor is there any end in sight. The court is determined to go farther and farther Right, taking the Constitution with it.

In the term just ended, the court time and time again decided 5-4 in favor of retrograde policies. It ruled that:

• Public money could go for vouchers for religious school tuition in clear violation of the separation of church and state.

• Schools may drug-test students engaged in extracurricular activities, including chess players and chorus members.

• States are immune from suits over legitimate complaints brought by federal agencies.

• Employees need not pay back wages to undocumented workers, one of many rulings favoring business over workers.

• Private prisons cannot be sued for imposing cruel and unusual punishment on inmates.

• Law officers may search bus passengers even though they had never been told of their Miranda rights.

• A prison program is constitutional even though it forces inmates to confess their crimes or be placed in a maximum security facility, a clear violation of the Fifth Amendment.

To show just how political the Supreme Court has become, President Bush took to the stump with an effusive speech lauding the vouchers decision as "just as historic" as the Brown desegregation decision. The far-fetched comparison shows once again that Bush's ignorance is vast.

More reactionaryism. The court continues to display extreme hostility to labor. After one decision this term, The

Nation lamented that the court majority "lives in denial of the social reality millions of working people face every day."

Recalling a case the Retrograde Five decided previously, The Nation noted that "millions of undocumented workers lost the right to be reinstated to their jobs if they were fired for joining a union."

The decision encouraged firms to continue stopping organizing among immigrant workers. In 31 percent of union drives, employers illegally fire workers, immigrant and native-born alike. This violates federal law.

Then this term the court ruled for employers in three cases under the Americans with Disabilities Act.

In another 5-4 decision, the court struck down a Minnesota law that barred judicial candidates from speaking out "on disputed legal or political issues." This might seem like a First Amendment victory. It is not. Judicial elections are an abomination. States have a right to curb judicial candidates' speech.

As Justice Ginsburg noted in dissent: the office of judges "is to administer justice." Judges are not political actors, she said, so states can safeguard the integrity of the system.

Amid the gross constitutional retreat of the Reactionary Five, the court did made a few good decisions. It took a small step toward eliminating the death penalty—what Pope John Paul II rightly calls the culture of death—by barring the execution of the mentally retarded. America is one of just three nations that permit such executions. (The others are Japan and Kyrgyzstan.)

The court rightly ruled that land use and zoning regulations to control growth at Lake Tahoe were essential to preserve environmental health. It rightly declared unconstitutional a law against making "virtual" child pornography, a victory for free speech on the Web.

It struck down an Ohio village ordinance that forbade door-to-door advocacy without first getting permission from city hall. It was a constitutional triumph for the Jehovah's Witnesses in their constant battle against the tyranny of the majority.

Among the most outrageous statements were:

• Justice Thomas saying handcuffing prisoners to a metal pole for hours in brutal summer heat was "for a legitimate penological purpose: encouraging…compliance with prison rules."

• Justice Scalia, writing the majority 5-4 opinion upholding the death sentence of an inmate whose court-appointed lawyer had represented the murder victim, calling it a "mere theoretical division of loyalty."

• Chief Justice Rehnquist, dissenting in the Jehovah's Witnesses case, saying the village need not "first endure its own crime wave before it takes measures to prevent crime."

Americans have an undue reverence for the Supreme Court. They do not realize how political and reactionary the court has become.

Sparks Tribune, Aug. 1, 2002

Supreme Court stuns

The ever rightward march of the U.S. Supreme Court has been checked by two momentous decisions. One upheld affirmative action and the other struck down a Texas sodomy law.

The affirmative action decision means it is constitutional for Michigan law school to consider race in admissions. The sodomy decision means government cannot criminalize private sexual behavior.

The liberal rulings to end the 2002-2003 term were amazing coming from the reactionary Rehnquist Court. But the reason is simple: Justice O'Connor. She refused to join Chief Justice Rehnquist and Justices Scalia and Thomas in their 16th century thinking.

Her vote in the affirmative action case proved pivotal. In the majority opinion, O'Connor called affirmative action close to a moral imperative. She noted that universities train society's leaders and that a society with racial and ethnic tensions benefits tremendously from an integrated leadership.

O'Connor was impressed by the friend-of-the-court briefs filed by retired generals and powerful Fortune 500 companies. They pointed out that an increasingly diverse nation and ever-more globalization demand preservation of affirmative action.

Unfortunately, the court invalidated the university's undergraduate affirmative action program. The majority did not see the case with the clarity of Justice Ginsburg in dissent. She rightly complained of the inequality in America, rightly noting that race still matters in housing, health care, income and schooling.

As Ginzburg pointed out, it is conservative sophistry, with its cry of "colorblindness," to denounce affirmative action. Affirmative action doesn't begin to compare with centuries of oppression, destruction and discrimination. It does not begin to overcome the horrors of 250 years of slavery and one hundred years of Jim Crow.

O'Connor's vote in the sodomy case, plus that of Justice Kennedy, was instrumental in the gay liberation decision. The court toppled its infamous 1986 Hardwick ruling that upheld Georgia's antisodomy law.

"Liberty presumes an autonomy of self that includes freedom of thought, belief, expression and certain intimate conduct," Kennedy said in the majority opinion.

Government cannot demean gays and lesbians by making their sexual conduct a crime. Government may not impose its moral code. Government cannot deprive gays of their humanity. Government cannot strip their right to "retain their dignity" as free people.

Kennedy cited the 1981 opinion of the European Court of Human Rights, calling it an example of an emerging Western consensus on sexual privacy. O'Connor, in a separate opinion, cited equal protection. She said government cannot make conduct for gays impermissable while allowing it for hetrosexuals.

Homosexuality is not deviant behavoir, it is not immoral and it is not a sin. The decision was summed up neatly by columnist E.J. Dionne: "a Magna Carta of gay rights."

O'Connor, in further proof that she refuses to jump out the window with the reactionaries, voted to uphold a national program channeling millions of dollars annually for legal services for the poor. She also supplied the swing vote in a decision that struck down California's unconstitutional effort to erase statutes of limitations retroactively for people accused of sexual molestation.

Unfortunately, O'Connor reverted to type when the court upheld California's barbarous three-strikes-and-you're-out law. O'Connor, once a prosecutor in Arizona, joined the reactionary bloc to provide the typical 5-4 injustice. It was the court's most horrendous decision of the term.

She lamely suggested that any criticism of the law should be directed at the California legislature. But legislatures, wanting to be perceived as tough on crime, simply will not revoke a law that it is clearly cruel and unusual punishment barred by the Eighth Amendment.

So California can put a man away for 25 years for stealing three golf clubs from a pro shop and 50 years for a man stealing nine videotapes from a Kmart. Their previous two offenses were minor. But none of that mattered to the hanging justices, totally unmindful that murderers do far less time.

Justice Souter, in dissent, called the sentence in the videotape theft what it is: grossly disproportionate. Justice Breyer, in dissent, called the sentence in the golf club case what it is: "unique in its harshness."

The court also returned to its draconian ways by upholding restrictions on prison visitation rights in Michigan, forbidding family visits for two years if an inmate commits two drug or alcohol violations.

Overall, however, the court moved away from the extreme right in two highly important cases. The irony is that conservatives like O'Connor and Kennedy now may be perceived as centrists.

Sparks Tribune, July 10, 2003

Vouchers ruling batters Constitution

It is hardly surprising that the worst Supreme Court in history has upheld school vouchers. As usual, this reactionary court found its right-wing politics in the Constitution.

Vouchers had been rightly declared unconstitutional by the federal district court and the appeals court. Both courts agreed that taxpayer support for religious schools was a clear breach of the wall of separation between church and state.

The district judge in Cleveland, noting that nearly all the students receiving vouchers attend parochial schools, said "a program that is so skewed toward religion necessarily results in indoctrination…and provides financial incentives to attend religious schools."

The 6th U.S. Circuit Court of Appeals in Cincinnati, upholding the district court, said: "The scheme involves the grant of state aid…to the coffers of…religious schools. It is unquestioned that these institutions incorporate religious concepts, motives and themes into all facets of their (schooling)."

But the Ideological Five reversed the lower courts, toppling precedent and rewriting the Constitution to fit its pro-voucher, reactionary view. The ruling is a devastating blow to the democratic notion of public schooling. Moreover, it is part of a dangerous worldwide trend to privatization.

Vouchers and privatization have been part of the right-wing agenda for a decade. President Bush and his fellow ideologues on the court are chortling now because they can impose their misbegotten policies.

While some people, particularly inner city blacks, see vouchers as an appealing school choice, they are a horrible breach of the sacred First Amendment. The answer to the faltering public school system is spending more money to repair its ills without tearing down the wall of separation that Jefferson knew was so essential.

Public schools are underfunded, overcrowded and poorly maintained. Vouchers siphon off money that could bolster the public schools, fix those problems and get better teachers and buy computers and textbooks.

As E.J. Dionne, Washington Post columnist, says: vouchers are "a form of cheap grace for those who want to pretend they care about poor kids even as they evade the cost of fixing the deep inequities built into our educational system."

True, parochial schools have rigorous academic teaching often lacking in public schools. But they put faith before reason. As George Bernard Shaw said: "A Catholic education is a contradiction in terms."

The five politicians on the court always manufacture reasons for their decisions. They confirm the old story about Chief Justice John Marshall. He gave his opinion to an associate justice, Joseph Story, and said, in effect: here is the law, now you find precedent for it.

The story, probably apocryphal, illustrates how justices can marshal legal arguments for any preconceived position. The law reads the way the Retrograde Five wants it to read, not what the Constitution says.

Justice Souter said as much in dissent. He quoted from the 1947 Everson case: "No tax in any amount, large or small, can be levied to support any religious activities or institutions, whatever they may be called or whatever form they may adopt to teach or practice religion."

He decried state aid going to "schools that can fairly be characterized as founded to teach religious doctrine and to imbue teaching in all subjects with a religious dimension."

Souter added: "Everson's statement is still the touchstone of sound law." But naturally the five reactionaries ignored Everson. They simply ruled as what they wanted to rule.

Barry Lynn, head of the Americans United for the Separation of Church and State, notes correctly that is not anti-Catholicism behind opposition to vouchers. Rather, people don't want "their money supporting a religion—any religion—that they don't believe in."

And who can blame them? Most parochial schools require their students to attend Mass and other religious ceremonies. Taxpayer money goes to buy Bibles, crucifixes and prayer books—an intolerant insult to the public.

Social critic Wendy Kaminer sees vouchers as teaching bias: "By directing government funds to parochial schools, vouchers will entangle government in sectarianism, forcing taxpayers to support religious ideas and practices—and religious bigotry—that are anathema to them."

The Retrograde Five are: Chief Justice Rehnquist and Justices Scalia, Thomas, O'Connor and Kennedy.

May they live in infamy.

Sparks Tribune, July 28, 2002

Antediluvian justices

The U. S. Supreme Court has had just 108 members over 214 years. Most have been nonentities, about 10 have been reactionaries and about 15 make any historian's list of judicial all-stars. But none has been as odious and dinosauristic as Justices Scalia and Thomas.

Scalia exudes Old Testament God of wrath compared with New Testament compassion of Christ. Thomas is a case for psychologists, better suited to be a justice of peace than a Supreme Court justice.

In the term just completed, the court stuck down an obnoxious Texas anti-sodomy law. But Scalia raved in dissent that the court had "taken sides in the culture war," that it was advancing the homosexual agenda, that it was inventing a new constitutional right by a court "impatient of democratic change."

Then, summoning up what lawyers call "the parade of horribles," Scalia railed against "a massive disruption of the social order": laws limiting marriage to hetrosexuals and barring bigamy, prostitution and incest. He raised a grim specter: "Every single one of these laws is called into question by today's decision."

He insisted that repealing laws against homosexual sodomy was the job of legislatures, not the courts, because "those judgments are to be made by the people and not imposed by a governing caste that knows best." (Those were not the sentiments of Scalia when he voted to hand the presidency to George W. Bush by stopping a Florida vote recount.)

Thomas called the Texas sodomy law uncommonly silly but said in dissent that he could not find privacy in the Constitution and therefore the people should decide.

Scalia and Thomas should read the stirring words of Justice Jackson in West Virginia State Board of Education v. Barnette (1943). Writing some of the finest words ever put into a Supreme Court opinion, Jackson pointed out that fundamental rights should never be put to a vote:

"The very purpose of a Bill of Rights was to withdraw certain subjects from the vicissitudes of political controversy, to place them beyond the reach of majorities and officials and to establish them as legal principles to be applied by the courts. One's right to life, liberty and property, to free speech, a free press, freedom of worship and assembly and other fundamental rights may not be submitted to vote. They depend on the outcome of no elections."

Courts must prevent the tyranny of the majority, they must act where legislators will not and they cannot wait for the people to grant minorites their basic rights and liberties.

Take flag burning. Twice the Supreme Court struck down as unconstitutional anti-flag burning laws overwhelmingly voted for by representatives of the people in Texas and Congress. Take desegregation. Alabama and Mississippi would still have segregated schools if not outlawed by the Supreme Court.

In another landmark decision, the court upheld affirmative action for the Michigan law school. But Thomas, apparently suffering a guilty conscience because he got into Holy Cross and Yale law school via affirmative action, called affirmative action demeaning. In addition, he was appointed to the Supreme Court—although grossly unqualified—solely because he is black.

Thomas ranted that affirmative action was "a faddish slogan of the cognoscenti." All he wanted was "a chance to stand on his own legs" without the great harm he said was caused by affirmative action.

Columnist Maureen Dowd was so right to write: "It's impossible not to be disgusted by someone who could benefit so much from affirmative action and then pull the ladder up after himself." Or as Justice Marshall put it so well about Thomas: "goddamn black sellout."

Dowd also has Scalia dead to rights: an "Archie Bunker in a high-backed chair," a stegosaurus, fancying himself an intellectual, nostalgic for the days "when military institutes did not have to accept women, when elite schools did not have to make special efforts with blacks and when a gay couple within their own bedroom could be clapped in irons."

Dissenting in the decision to uphold the channeling of funds for legal aid, Scalia complained that the court had endorsed a "Robin Hood taking," taking "from the rich to give to indigent defendants…a larcenous beneficence."

As for being intellectual, what intellectual could write: "We are fools for Christ's sake. We must pray for the courage to endure the scorn of the sophisticated world"?

The Constitution means what these two reactionaries say it means. Sadly, it is not the Constitution that many Americans cherish.

Sparks Tribune, July 17, 2003

Good athlete, poor justice

One of the worst things John F. Kennedy ever did as president was to appoint Byron "Whizzer" White to the Supreme Court.

He did so because White was a friend from Oxford days and they had established a bond as Navy lieutenants in the Pacific during World War II. But the judicial career of White shows that palship is hardly qualification for a court that determines the constitutional law of the land.

The truth is that White was a poor justice, not the worst ever to serve on the court, but a mediocrity who was far too conservative. The virtual silence of commentors and columnists on his death in April indicated as much.

Indeed, White was a better football player than a justice. (He was an All-America at Colorado and National Football League rookie of the year in 1938.) A purported Democrat, he was little more than a Kennedyophile.

White dissented shamefully in two landmark cases: the Roe v. Wade abortion decision of 1973 and the 1966 Miranda's decision giving suspects the right to remain silent and consult a lawyer.

In Roe, which liberated women from the burden of unwanted children, White was one of just two dissenters. He complained in Roe of "raw judicial power...an improvident and extravagant exercise of judicial review."

In Miranda he argued that suspects' right to remain silent would make it too difficult for police to extract confessions. (Presumably at the end of rubber hoses that had served the police so well in exacting false confessions.)

In Hardwick in 1986, White cast the deciding vote that upheld the absurd Georgia statute banning sodomy. His opinion called the constitutional right to engage in homosexual sex facetious.

He often voted against affirmative action. He often

wrote majority opinions that cut back on the scope of federal civil rights laws, drawing justifiably sharp criticism from civil rights groups.

He usually supported the prosecution side in criminal cases, foolishly relying on the "good faith" of prosecutors. He sided with the government in battles with the press. He chipped away at Warren Court precedents.

In 1962 when the court struck down a California law that made it a crime for a person to be a narcotics addict because it violated the Eightth Amendment ban on cruel and unusual punishment, White dissented.

His opinion in the 1972 Branzburg case argued, wrongly, that journalists must disclose their confidential sources to a grand jury. He was so wrong, in fact, that the majority of states passed shield laws providing the protection that the media need.

He was anything but "the ideal New Frontier judge" that Kennedy called him. Still, anyone who served 31 years on the court as White did was bound to judge a few cases right.

In a 1991 case in which the majority upheld an Indiana law banning nude dancing, White dissented. He said nude dancing was protected by the First Amendment even though such dancing might not be high art. He rightly said: "The court's assessment of the artistic merits of nude dancing performances should not be the determining factor in deciding this case."

White's finest opinion was in First National Bank of Boston v. Bellotti in 1978. The Supreme Court invalidated a Massachusetts statute that prohibited business corporations from making expenditures to influence the vote on any question submitted to the voter other than one affecting the company.

The statute was upheld by the highest court in Massachusetts. But the U.S. Supreme Court called it unconstitutional, declaring that it went to "the heart of the First Amendment's protection."

White, in a dissent joined by Justices William Brennan and Thurgood Marshall, said the statute *protected* First Amendment rights. He rightly argued that corporations had amassed great wealth and thus could be prevented from having "an unfair advantage in the political process."

His conclusion was impeccable: "The use of communication as a means of self-expression, self-realization and self-fulfillment, is not at all furthered by corporate speech. It is clear that the communications of profitmaking corporations are not 'an integral part of the development of ideas, of mental exploration and of the affirmation of self.' "

Giving First Amendment protection to Big Bucks demeans that great writ. And White knew it. As Anatole France wrote: "The law, in its majestic equality, forbids the rich as well as the poor to sleep under bridges…and to steal bread."

Sparks Tribune, June 27, 2002

Supreme Court myth

Peter Irons has done for Supreme Court history what Howard Zinn has done for U.S. history: demythologizing it while highlighting its often shameful past.

Irons shows the truth behind a comment by a former chief justice: "the Constitution is what the judges say it is." And often what they *say* the Constitution says is not to be found in the text. The Constitution doesn't change—just the justices.

Raw politics often prevails over legal reason. Justices are more swayed by personal and political sentiments than by arguments. Then, these remarkable prestidigitators marshal opinions to support their predilections.

Of 108 justices in history, the vast majority have been mediocrities and non-entities who have found their conservative to reactionary views in the Constitution. They have been more politicians than judges.

These sour reflections are exemplified by today's Rehnquist Court, the most reactionary in history—even worse than the Four Horseman of Reaction who so bedeviled President Roosevelt in the 1930s.

Yet too few Americans know this reality. They have undue reverence for the court.

Irons, politicial science professor at the University of California, San Diego, readily admits that his "A People's History of the Supreme Court" is inspired by and modeled after Zinn's "A People's History of the United States."

As Zinn himself writes in the forward: "The justices of the Supreme Court are not simply black-robed repositories of objective wisdom. Rather...they come out of the political system, out of a social context and each brings to the court legal philosophies and moral attitudes that come out of (their) background."

The court has been dominated since its inception in

1789 by white men from the Establishment. It has ruled for the insiders, rather than the outsiders, for the status quo rather than for the people.

The first great chief justice, John Marshall, would conjure up opinions "almost from thin air." Irons notes that Marshall's opinions often made up in certitude what they lacked in substance. Marshall cited "plain meanings" of the Constitution which were not plain to anyone else. But they suited his politics. As Irons writes, Marshall "read the Constitution through the eyes of a committed and partisan Federalist."

Marshall was not the greatest chief justice, as is often said. Earl Warren was. Marshall put property above people. Warren put people above property. The difference is vast.

The worst decision of the Supreme Court was Dred Scott (1857)—or at least until the recent Bush v. Gore decision that made Bush an unelected president. (The Bush-Gore case was decided after the Irons book was published.)

The racist chief justice, Roger Taney, wrote a pro-slavery manifesto in Dred Scott: blacks were "an inferior order and altogether unfit to associate with the white race...They had no rights that the white man was bound to respect."

Moreover, "the negro might justly and lawfully be reduced to slavery for his own benefit." Blacks were not U.S. citizens and could not claim "rights and privileges" even if their masters took them to free territories. (So much for Jefferson's declaration "that all men are created equal.")

"Taney twisted legal precedent and bent the Consititution out of shape, all to achieve his predetermined goal of promoting the extension of slavery into the territories," Irons writes.

Another disgraceful decision upheld Jim Crow. That court ruling in 1896 was "second only to Dred Scott in Supreme Court infamy," Irons notes.

The court was terribly wrong in Schenck (1919) when it upheld a conviction for distributing pamphlets against the war and calling conscription a violation of the 13th Amendment bar to slavery.

Justice Oliver Wendell Holmes wrote for the court words that have a modern echo today when it has become treason to reason: "When a nation is at war many things that might be said in times of peace are such a hindrance to its effort that no court could regard them as protected by any constitutional right."

Holmes treated the great socialist, Eugene Debs, as a common criminal for giving an anti-war speech, a speech that clearly deserved First Amendment protection. (So much for Wilson's pledge to make the world safe for democracy.)

"In all the history of the country, the working class has never named a federal judge," Debs said. All too true.

The justices usually rule for the conservative lawyer class, not the people. All too few justices have been like Louis Brandeis: a "dangerously radical" people's lawyer before he got on the court and a people's justice on the court.

Sparks Tribune, May 1, 2003

Rightly tossing God from Pledge

The public howled, the politicians genuflected and the president pontificated over the ruling by a federal court that the words under God in the Pledge of Allegiance are unconstitutional.

Such fealty to God is hardly surprising. This is a country that fervently believes the interests of the nation are God's interests. But the vast bulk of people and politicians are dead wrong.

God should not be on the country's banner. Church and state must be forever separate. Religion is a matter of private conscience. It is not the business of government.

The spectacle in the House and Senate was ridiculous, with gross pandering to the public. The senators showed up *en masse* for morning prayer after the ruling, bowed their heads and declared that this was "one nation under God." Meanwhile, nearly all 435 representatives gathered to recite the pledge—some even shouting "under God."

President Bush, calling America a nation that values its "relationship with the Almighty," said the country needs "common-sense judges" who understand that the rights of the people are "derived from God."

One disgraceful politician, Rep. Joseph Pitts of Pennsylvania, hyperventilated, declaring that democracy is threatened by such rulings. And Sen. Harry Byrd of West Virginia showed his stupid side by calling the two judges in the majority stupid.

Sure, politicians know the politic thing to do. Roughly 97 percent of the American people believe in God. So politicians must blather about God.

They are on the right side of public sentiment but on the wrong side of the Constitution and the wrong side of reason and truth. Yet in this country, a candidate declaring he was an atheist could not even get elected dogcatcher.

In a 2-1 vote, the 9th U.S. Circuit Court of Appeals ruled that the pledge could not be recited in schools because it violated the First Amendment prohibition against a state endorsement of religion.

Look, the pledge is mumbled by rote. Most kids neither know what the words mean nor what is being said. They often misconstrue the words. Columnist Rob Morse of the San Francisco Chronicle wrote that as a schoolboy he was swearing "a legion" to someone named Richard Stans "under guard."

The pledge was added by Congress in 1954 with little discussion and by voice vote. The Cold War was at its peak and "godless communism" was the enemy. (The Soviets were right intellectually to get rid of God but wrong politically. Most people need a deity no matter how defined.)

The New York Times carried a page one story recently saying the Ninth Circuit is developing "a reputation for being wrong more often than any other appeals court."

No. It is the Supreme Court that is wrong. The Ninth Circuit, based in San Francisco, is the most progressive court in the land. The Supreme Court is reactionary.

Justice William Brennan would have agreed with the pledge ruling. His fellow Catholic parishioners were so incensed after his pro-abortion vote in Roe v. Wade that he had to change parishes. But Brennan's eye was on the Constitution not on the Vatican abortion position.

With similar clarity, Brennan dissented in 1983 in a 6-3 Supreme Court decision upholding congressional and state legislative prayer. He called such prayer what it is: unconstitutional.

"If the court were to judge legislative prayer through the unsentimental eye of our settled doctrine, it would have to strike it down as a clear violation of the Establishment Clause. (That clause: 'Congress shall make no law respecting an establishment of religion.')

"The Establishment Clause embodies a judgment born of long and turbulent history that in our society religion 'must be private matter for the individual.' "

Brennan rightly argued that prayer is no business of government, that the wall of separation between church and state must never be breached.

As for the "formulaic recitation of 'God save the United States and this Honorable Court,' used to open Supreme Court proceedings, and the slogan printed on money, "In God We Trust," Brennan said, "they have lost any true religious significance."

Brennan rightly concluded: "If the court had struck down legislative prayer, it would likely have stimulated a furious reaction. But it would also...have invigorated both the spirit of religion and the spirit of freedom."

Freedom for some Americans, despite the yowling of politicians and the keening of the masses, is freedom *from* religion.

Sparks Tribune, July 11, 2002

Bush court-packing

The Bush administration desperately seeks to pack the federal courts with right-wing ideologues. The Senate is just as adamant about rejecting judicial nominees totally unfit to be federal judges.

Leon Holmes, named to federal district court in Arkansas, has said: "the woman is to place herself under the authority of the man...A wife is to subordinate herself to her husband." He also has written that "abortion should not be available to rape victims because conceptions from rape occur with the same frequency as snow in Miami."

Such thinking is worthy of the 17th century. It is not thinking that belongs on the bench in the 21st century. It is a reactionary view that even many Republicans reject.

Here's another antediluvian President Bush wants on the appellate court: Charles Pickering. (Bush spouts fine words about black equality, pats black kids on the head for photo ops but names racist judges.)

Bush would put Pickering on the 5th U.S. Circuit of Appeals in New Orleans despite his segregationist record. Pickering called a cross-burning case just a "drunken prank." Pickering opposes abortion, advocates strengthening the law against miscegenation and voted as a state senator to fund the segregationist Sovereignty Commission.

• Another bad choice by Bush: William Pryor. Pryor, Alabama attorney general, has been nominated to the appeals court in Atlanta. He has urged a greater role for Christianity in public life. He denounces Roe as "the worst abomination of constitutional law in our history." He defends a Ten Commandments monument in Alabama's court building. Stooping to demogogic politics, the GOP circulated a viscious lying ad: he's being opposed because he is a Catholic. Some of Pryor's foes are Catholics.

• And another: Jeffrey Sutton. He is the nominee to

the 6th U.S. Circuit Court of Appeals in Cincinnati. Sutton is an advocate of state's rights who is still fighting the Civil War. He urged the Supreme Court to deprive millions of workers of legal protection. He opposed the Violence Against Women Act.

• And another: Miguel Estrada. He was named to the appeals court in Washington, D.C. Brilliant political appointment. Latino name. But Estrada is so conservative that even Latino groups oppose his nomination. Moreover, Estrada is so adept at hiding his views that he is rightly called a stealth candidate.

• And another: Carolyn Kuhl. Bush wants to put her on the 9th circuit appeals court. She urges that Roe v. Wade be overturned. She urged tax exempt status for Bob Jones University even though it has discriminated against blacks.

• And still another: Janis Brown. She has been named to the U.S. Court of Appeals for the District of Columbia. As a justice of the California Supreme Court, Brown supports limitations on abortion rights, would ease corporate liability, favors the death penalty, opposes gun controls and rejects affirmative action.

• And yet another: Deborah Cook. Named to the 6th circuit appeals court. On the Ohio Supreme Court, Cook ruled against injured workers, discrimination victims and consumers. She sides with Big Business and insurance firms. She rules for discriminating firms, abusive bosses and employers who injure their workers and then lie about it.

• Then still another: Priscilla Owens. On the Texas Supreme Court she has voted against workers and accident victims. She says a minor must prove that she is aware of religious objections to abortion.

All those nominees are types that Bush would love to put on the Supreme Court. The tragedy, if they would be confirmed, is that their reactionary views would plague the courts long after Bush leaves office.

179

Bush is salivating over a potential Supreme Court nomination, enabling him to pick the fifth justice needed to overthrow Roe v. Wade. And who is President Bush's favorite Supreme Court justice? Antonin Scalia, the most reactionary justice in U.S. history.

Scalia favors anti-sodomy laws, votes against admitting women to VMI, votes against affirmative action, complains about legal aid to the poor, supports blue laws keeping stores closed on Sundays, opposes abortion, rebukes liberal judges who "have found rights where society never believed they existed" and complains of affirmative action. Nor does he see anything cruel and unusual about clapping a man behind bars for life for possessing 672 grams of cocaine.

Scalia and his ilk would outright-wing the despicable right-wing.

Sparks Tribune, Aug. 28, 2003

History

Reasons behind 9/11

America, the Land of Excess.

The media, in an upsurge of sentiment and patriotism, poured out millions of words and devoted hours of footage to the first anniversary of 9/11. The overkill was manifest.

The San Francisco Chronicle came out with black borders on pages, a symbol of mourning used by newspapers of yesteryear, a practice thought to have been long dead. The Chronicle ran melodramatic headlines: "9/11. Voices. Epilogue. Our Readers Reflect. YEARNING FOR A BETTER WORLD."

Ballparks all over America plastered on outfield fences, scoreboards, lineup cards and T-shirts this message: "We shall not forget." Life magazine produced a 9/11 heirloom edition with a satin-ribbon page marker "accented with pure 22 kt gold and crafted to last for generations."

America loves to wax maudlin on anniversaries. Even many New Yorkers sickened at the excessive memoralizing. As Steven Mikulan of LA Weekly wrote: "Many New Yorkers…are fed up with the media's endless stream of stories of memorial quilts, hero dogs or how 9/11 affected a small Midwestern town."

But Rob Morse, Chron columnist, did not run with the herd as people did in the Ionesco play "Rhinoceros." Morse wrote on 9/11/02: "Most of you want to escape the tearjerker music and video of flames and dust. The media and the politicians have gone too far. We're just one step away from making this date a national holiday."

None of this is to condone the heinous events of 9/11. But almost no columnist or politician explained to the American people the whys behind the terrorist attack. Nor did they examine the terrible role played by the United States in history.

George Orwell wrote that he had the "power of facing

unpleasant facts." Americans must face unpleasant facts, facts more telling than emotion.

America was targeted on 9/11 because of its constant one-sided support of Israel and backing of Israeli settlements on Palestinian soil, its pervasive military presence in the Mideast and throughout the world and its support for autocratic regimes in Saudi Arabia and Kuwait.

Insufficient justification? Perhaps not. But there is no doubt that it was retribution for an American history that reeks of crimes against humanity. Even a casual reading of that history indicates that in 9/11 the chickens were coming home to roost, as Malcolm X said after the John F. Kennedy assassination.

The historic crimes of the United States include: the slaughter and ouster of the Indians from their land; constitutional covenant with slavery; the seizure of Mexican land in the Southwest; slaughter of Filipinos; countless invasions; overthrow of governments and political assassinations; the mad bomber Henry Kissinger, war criminal *par excellence*; support for murderous dictators; backing of nations using death squads; and what Nation magazine called "the sordid history of U.S. involvement in Iran, Guatemala, Vietnam, Chile, East Timor and Nicaragua."

America masterminded the killing of Allende and supported the killer Pinochet. It backed mass murder in Indonesia. It invaded Panama in violation of international law and kidnapped Noreiga.

It engineered a coup that overthrew the leftish Mossadegh in Iran and installed the rightist Shah. CIA crimes include terrorism, assassination, torture and violations of human rights. The CIA trained and armed death squads in Guatemala.

Should this record make Americans swell with pride? Should Americans be proud that the wealthiest nation in the world does not have the cradle-to-grave socialism of civilized countries like Sweden? That America has no national health plan, no child care, no paid maternal leave? That it has the barbarous death penalty? That it ignores the wisdom of the world in regard to treaties? That it ravages the environment?

America has one law for itself and another for the rest of the world. America does what it wants. It is has been an imperial bully, not an innocent victim. It has so much hubris that it feels it has the right to invade any country, anywhere under any pretext.

Talk of a better world? The United States has so often prevented the world from being better. America changed forever by 9/11? Nonsense. Is the nation any kinder? Is the nation any the less imperial, unilateral? Does it flaunt any the less its military prowess, visiting death and destruction in the world? Is it any the less a rogue, terroristic nation?

The answer to the question, "Why do they hate us?" is simple. 9/11, as dreadful as it was, was partial payback for centuries of American wrongs.

Sparks Tribune, Oct. 10, 2002

King George makes war

Much of the world is against a U.S. invasion of Iraq. Huge numbers of the American people are opposed as proved by the largest antiwar demonstrations ever. But the opinion of just one man counts: that of King George. Bush is taking America to war—to his everlasting shame.

The arrogance of President Bush is colossal. "I'm the commander," he says. "See, I don't have to explain why I say things…I don't feel like I owe anybody an explanation."

No matter that this is an unjust, unconstitutional and unnecessary war, a war that violates international law. Bush bullies, threatens, bribes, cajoles and blackmails other nations to get on the U.S. side. Bush is the world threat—not Saddam Hussein.

Under the outrageous Bush Doctrine, the United States can invade any nation at any time under the flimiest pretexts. The Bush obsession borders on madness. He was thirsting for this war for a year. No matter that all the facts are against war.

First, Bush argues regime change—but only regimes he finds evil. Then he talks about weapons of mass destruction. (Many nations have them). Then he sees a non-existent link to Al Qaeda. Then he wants to bring democracy to Iraq. (No Arab country is a democracy.)

His latest "reason" is that Iraq poses a threat to U.S. security. Nonsense. For 12 years America has battered Iraq with low-level warfare including a no-fly zone and a cruel embargo.

No matter that France and Russia would veto a Security Council resolution authorizing war in Iraq. No matter what the United Nations thinks. The U.N. is irrelevant to bellicose Bush if it doesn't support America.

Meanwhile, the government will be even more niggardly about domestic needs. No matter that 75 million Americans are without health insurance. No matter that senior citizens need prescription drugs to be covered by Medicare. No matter that the schools are in disarray. No matter that the budget is busted, that tax cuts would mean a deficit of $1.82 trillion over the next decade. No matter that the economy is tanking, that joblessness is 5.8 percent and rising.

President John Quincy Adams said in 1821 that America does not go "abroad in search of monsters to destroy." Unfortunately, it has—and does.

Most U.S. wars have been unjust. President Polk waged war with Mexico over a phony pretext. President McKinley fought Spain in Cuba and the Philippines on false grounds. President Teddy Roosevelt sent an American warship to Colombia to seize the Panama Canal.

The United States engineered coups to overthrow Mossadegh in Iran, Arbenz in Guatemala and Allende in Chile. Its lists of invasions are appalling: Haiti, Panama, Grenada, Dominican Republic (twice)—and so many more. Its bombings are appalling: Libya, Laos, Cambodia, Vietnam, Bosnia, Sudan, Guatemala, Indonesia—and so many more.

This is supposed to be a peace-loving, always-right, exceptional, God-fearing, religious nation?

Recall that it was "the voice of God" that told McKinley to invade the Philippines, to educate, "uplift and Christianize" the people. Bush is also acting in the name of God, extolling God's master plan. His messiah complex leads him to believe that his mission is divine. He told the nation that it could place "confidence in the loving God behind all of life and all of history."

Reality checks:

• **John Kiesling**, career diplomat, resigned recently with this stinging blast: "We have not seen such systematic distortion of intelligence, such systematic manipulation of the American people, since the war in Vietnam."

• **Nelson Mandela**, former president of South Africa, said Bush is plunging "the world into a holocaust...Why does the United States behave so arrogantly? Their friend Israel has weapons of mass destruction...All it wants is Iraqi oil."

• **Howard Zinn**, great U.S historian: "Arguments for the war are paper thin and fall apart at first touch...The wife of the president calls off a gathering of poets in the White House because the poets have rebelled, seeing the march to war as a violation of the most sacred values of poets through the ages."

• **Kurt Vonnegut,** author of the classic "Slaughterhouse Five," lamented on his 80th birthday: "I'm mad about being old and I'm mad about being American." Getting old is damnable—a shipwreck, as de Gaulle put it. But worse is the folly of war without just cause.

Bush gives every sign of being a one-term president. Perhaps the wish is father to the thought. But his abhorrent domestic policies and disastrous foreign policy should defeat him in 2004.

Sparks Tribune, March 13, 2003

Class warfare rampant

Few will say it—and certainly no politician—but the United States has been in class warfare almost from the beginning of the Republic. We do not have a democracy. We have a plutocracy.

As Lewis Lapham, editor of Harper's, pointed out in an article on the Bush II administration:

"How else to describe the administration—elimination of the inheritance tax, revision of the bankruptcy laws, the repeal of safety regulations in the workplace, easing of restrictions on monopoly—except as acts of class warfare?"

Kevin Phillips makes clear in his important book, "Wealth and Democracy," that America has had a class war from its inception.

The American Revolution gained independence from Britain. But it was in no sense a social and economic revolution. Many signers of the Declaration of Independence were rich. And their great wealth often flowed from closeness to government. Aristocrats ruled. Slavery blemished the nascent nation.

The Phillips book is a must for those who deny that America, so-called land of equality, is really a land of class warfare. Watered stock—phantom value—was rampant in 1870 just as Enron, WorldCom, Global Cross *et al* watered stock in our day.

The Balzac dictum is mostly true: "Behind every great fortune there is a crime." (Read the criminal history of the Du Ponts of Delaware.)

Social Darwinism prevailed in the Gilded Age of robber barons at the end of the 19th century as it prevails today. Look no farther than the Bush tax cut that benefit 1 percent of the people—the rich.

That is class warfare.

Business tax favoritism. Allowing business to avoid

taxes by setting up dummy headquarters outside the United States. Industry bailouts. Lax regulation on corporations. Insider trading—which Bush himself was guilty of when in the corporate world.

That is class warfare.

By 2000 ordinary Americans were left behind. But *corporate* welfare is staggering: $60 billion in industry tax breaks and $75 billion in business subsidies yearly.

Class warfare.

Money rules politics and hence government. It is government by the corporations for corporations. Wall Street *über alles*.

The so-called tax reform of 1986 greatly reduced the progressivity of the income tax, dropping the highest bracket to 28 percent. Meanwhile, the regressive Social Security and Medicare payroll taxes were increased.

As Phillips writes: not even a huge book could do justice to the role of income taxation in "shaping, favoring and realigning wealth" in America.

This class warfare was abetted by reactionary supreme courts. The Supreme Court found for the railroads in 15 of 16 cases. It struck down an income tax law in 1894, calling it "an assault on capital," a war "of the poor against the rich." In 1923 it ruled against a minimum wage for women despite their abysmal pay and terribly long hours.

One look at the wealthy media empire goes a long way to explain its Mainstream slant: Cox, Newhouse, Hearst, Scripps, Murdoch and Turner.

Presidential primaries have become wealth primaries. Bush II beat John McCain, much better than Bush, because he steamrolled him with money. Al Gore pushed aside Bill Bradley, a more progressive candidate, because he piled up far more money.

Nationwide television advertising, requiring huge sums, means that money and TV have taken over elections.

Campaign contributions are nothing less than legalized bribery. Money for favors.

Presidential voter turnout, 49 percent in 2000, leads to selection of such reactionaires as Dubya Bush. Non-voters come from the less prosperous, Democratically-inclined ranks. The lower the turnout, the greater the class grip on government.

Moreover, so many working-class and lower middle-class people vote against their own economic interests. Why? Racism, homophobia. And, above all, presidential saber rattling.

British economist J.R. Hobson noted in 1902 that it had become commonplace to use wars to divert the populace from pressing domestic needs.

One hundred years later it still is true: we have the never-ending war on terrorism and the threat of war against Iraq to distract purported patriots from needed reforms.

Meanwhile, the rich get even richer. The poor get poorer. And the middle class must work furiously to stay even. It is class warfare.

Sparks Tribune, Aug. 29, 2002

Upside, downside of Carter

Jimmy Carter was a mediocre president but a great former president.

Most ex-presidents spend their time building libraries, writing memoirs and raising funds for their party. Not Carter.

As ex-president, he spent two decades peacemaking, battling for human rights, building houses, laboring on behalf of the poor, developing programs to control river blindness in Africa, fighting guinea-worm disease and monitoring elections.

Carter, who won the Nobel Peace Prize recently, was in the great tradition of sixth president John Quincy Adams. Adams spent two decades in the House of Representatives after serving in the White House, fighting an often lonely battle against slavery.

Carter's greatest achievement as president was securing the Panama Canal treaty. He did it over the strenuous objections of Ronald Reagan, who called it a giveaway and a mortal threat to U.S. security.

Teddy Roosevelt boasted that he seized the Panama Canal. It was just one of many affronts to Central American countries: U.S. invasions to protect United Fruit and its capitalistic ilk, coups and support for dictators.

Carter also shone in the White House by brokering the Camp David accords between Egypt's Anwar Sadat and Israel's Menachem Begin.

Among the 19 Americans who have won the peace prize was TR, a jingo of jingos, who got Japan and Russia to end their war in 1906. Another was Henry Kissinger, the war criminal. He was justly vilified for unleashing U.S. bombers on Vietnam, Cambodia and Laos.

Which leads to the terrible downside of the Carter presidency.

He inflated the military budget. He hobnobbed with

despots like the Shah. He restored the Khmer Rouge after the Vietnamese kicked it out of Cambodia; dispatched arms to the genocidal Indonesians; backed the South Korean military in its Kwanju massacre of 1,000; sided with the Salvadoran military in its brutal repression that killed thousands of peasants and workers; funded the anti-Soviets in Afghanistan; and ordered the CIA to train Nicaraguan contras against the leftist Sandinistas who had overthrown the dictator Somoza.

The Carter legacy is marred by other things. Namely: foolishness about his MX plan to shuttle missiles by rail across the Great Basin. And more foolishness about reinstituting registration for the draft. And still more foolishness: micromanaging the presidency to the extent of overseeing such trivial detail as construction of a White House tennis court.

Still, as president, Carter rightly urged Americans to shake the "inordinate fear of communism," a phobia that led to the evil of Joe McCarthy and a penchant for seeing communists under every bed. Later, Carter opposed the absurd political pundits who dismissed glasnost as a hoax to lull the West to sleep.

Carter also deserves high marks for opposing the Bush II warmongering over Iraq. Also: for opposing Bush's maintenance of the cruel embargo in Cuba solely for crass political reasons: winning Florida elections. Carter, visiting Havana, rightly paid homage to President Fidel Castro.

Carter also brought to the presidency a winning simplity: waving off the presidential limo to walk down Pennsylvania Avenue to his inauguration in 1977, hand in hand with his beloved wife Rosalynn. This was a throwback to Jefferson who walked to his first inauguration in 1801 from a boarding house.

Carter also appeared in the Oval Office wearing a sweater. And once as president he carried his own luggage, disdaining the Imperial Presidency. (His aides wrongly convinced him that this was undignified.)

Carter showed his rectitude and above-politics stance as far back as his inauguration as governor of Georgia in 1970. The Crackers assumed he was a segregationist. Carter rightly proclaimed that he favored integration.

But in the White House, Carter had bad luck: the energy crisis and the seizure of hostages. In contrast, a far, far unworthier man, Bush II, has had the enormous good luck to have had 9/11 and terrorism overshadow his reactionary and frightfully probusiness policies.

Carter was decent, ethical, upright, moral, honest and true. A good man. The nation has not had too many men of his character and integrity in the White House.

Carter's initials were J.C. Sometimes he acted in the White House more like Jesus Christ than Mr. President. Still, he was a humane man who could admit to an interviewer that he lusted after women in his heart.

Sparks Tribune, Dec. 12, 2002

Mallory and Everest

George Mallory is looming ever larger in the Mount Everest saga.

Everest, which Mallory may have summitted in 1924, seems now almost like a paved road. It has been crested 1,650 times since the first successful recorded climb in 1953.

Climbing expeditions these days are organized with military precision. Expert mountaineers can lead you to the top for $50,000. But admiration for Mallory is magnified by the contrast between his primitive climbing gear and the superequipment of today.

It's like comparing the crude state of photography that Mathew B. Brady used to record the Civil War with modern photo technology. Or, comparing the quill pen used by 18th century writers with writing on a computer.

Mallory had 33-pound oxygen tanks, clumsy and heavy compared with equipment used today. Audrey Salkeld, writing for Nova online, notes:

"For its day, going to Everest was like going to the moon. The small, ill-equipped little (Mallory) band dressed in an assortment of tweeds and homeknits, challenged Himalayan heights with little to assist them but indomitable spirit."

Today Everest climbers have the aid of ladders, fixed ropes and anchors never dreamed of by Mallory.

These thoughts about Mallory were prompted by the 50th anniversary last month of the first official ascent by Edmund Hillary, New Zealand beekeeper, and Tenzing Norgay, Nepalese Sherpa.

Hillary's son, Peter, triumphantly called recently by satellite phone. "Dad, it's Peter. We're on the summit." Peter's climb to mark the anniversary was filmed during a National Geographic expedition.

There may be more difficult mountains to climb than Everest. But none is more demanding physically and psychologically. Brutal winds. Intense cold. Frostbite. Oxygen starvation. Treacherous ice. Blinding snow. Hidden crevasses. Sudden, violent weather changes. More than five miles above sea level—29,035 feet to the summit. Absolutely forbidding, absolutely formidable—the ulimate physiological challenge.

But it's not just the climbing skill required, the physical conditioning. It's the debilitation caused by oxygen deprivation. A New York Times graphic illustrated that peril:

• Climbers near the summit have 70 percent less oxygen than they would at sea level.

• Climbers brought to the altitude of the death zone (25,000 feet) directly from sea level would die of oxygen starvation in a few minutes.

• "At extreme altitude, judgment is impaired and rapid physical deterioration sets in. Sometimes body fluids start filling lungs or cause the brain to swell, leading to a life-threatening condition."

The British Mallory and co-climber Andy Irvine were last seen disappearing in a swirl of mist near the summit. Did they fall ascending or descending?

John Williamson, former president of the American Alpine Club, thinks they reached the summit based on a sighting by Mallory teammate Noel Odell. In his "The Fight for Everest," Odell writes: "There is a strong probability that Mallory and Irvine succeeded."

Robert Graves thought so too. Graves was a friend of Mallory and author of the historical novel, "I, Claudius," which was made into a magnificent TV series starring Derek Jacobi.

In his 1929 memoir, "Goodbye to All That," Graves recalled how Mallory once made what he called an inexplicable, "impossible" climb on Mount Snowden in Wales. (Snowdon is a mere 3,560 feet. It is so easy to walk up that one-half million folks do it annually.)

"Anyone who has climbed with George is convinced that he got to the summit," Graves wrote. Mallory had "almost foolhardy daring yet he knew all there could be known about mountaineering technique. I always felt absolutely safe with him on the rope."

Graves also noted that Mallory, "who used to go drunk with excitement at the end of his climbs," took to mountain- and rock-climbing as a corrective to a weak heart.

Climbing Everest, between Nepal and Tibet, would be nearly impossible without the valiant Sherpas. They carry the vast majority of expedition supplies and set up camps. Yet they get little credit.

Jamling Norgay, son of Tensing who summitted Everest with Peter Hillary, called the Sherpas the "unsung heroes of Everest." More than 50 Sherpas have died on Everest and many more have been crippled. (Everest is Chomolongma in the Serpa tongue, "goddess mother of the snow.")

On a lecture tour of America in 1923, Mallory told Harvard students that he climbed Everest "for the spirit of adventure to keep alive the soul of man." More famously he answered the question of why climb Everest: "Because it's there."

Sparks Tribune, June 12, 2003

In praise of Du Bois

The lives of Frederick Douglass and W.E.B Du Bois are so often parallel. Both fought racism. Both felt the terrible stings to a man's soul because he was black in a white world. Both denounced the all-too-prevalent notion that blacks were inferior. And both overcame huge obstacles.

Douglass (1817-1895) was a writer, orator, newspaper editor and abolitionist. Du Bois (1868-1963) was a writer, historian, scholar, educator and civil rights leader. Both knew that the road to real freedom for blacks was education.

In the North Star for Jan. 8, 1848, Douglass wrote: "It must be no longer white lawyer and black woodsawyer, white editor and black street cleaner. It must be no longer white, intelligent and black, ignorant." Du Bois, "In the Souls of Black Folk," also acknowledges the necessity of education:

"The opposition to Negro education in the South was at first bitter and showed itself in ashes, insult and blood. For the South believed an educated Negro to be a dangerous Negro. And the South was not wholly wrong. For education among all kinds of men always has had and always will have an element of danger and revolution, of dissatisfaction and discontent."

This year has drawn special attention to Du Bois because it is the 100th anniversary of the publication of "The Souls of Black Folk." This collection of essays should be read by blacks *and whites*. It is a classic, often moving and sometimes even spiritual.

Unlike most PhDs, Du Bois could write. He tells the story of the struggle for civil rights and human rights. He tells why he frequently had an ache in his heart, how Jim Crow meant "slavery by other means". He makes present-day opposition to affirmative action seem so petty.

In an introduction to an anniversary edition, Henry Louis

Gates calls "Souls" an "urtext of the African-American experience," a "veritable touchstone of African-American culture for every successive generation of black scholars" and "almost as a cultural initiation rite" for black writers.

It is a must in black studies, yes. But as Felicia Lee asked earlier this year in an article in the New York Times: "When will Du Bois be embraced by America and be required reading for everyone?" No time soon, unfortunately.

Manning Marable, head of black history at Columbia, notes that the views of Du Bois, Martin Luther King and Malcolm X were made parochial rather than global, international and universal.

"It's like Martin Luther King frozen on the steps of the Lincoln Memorial saying 'I have a dream' but not seen protesting the Vietnam War or Malcolm saying 'by any means necessary' but not seen discussing using the U.N. to protest the condition of black Americans."

Both Douglass and Du Bois are heroes in black history. It is too fond a hope, however, that they will become heroes in American history anytime soon.

While Douglass had been a slave and later suffered horribly from discrimination, he was never buffeted by government as Du Bois was. Gates writes:

"Few American intellectuals have been treated with as much scorn and disrespect or harassed so relentlessly as Du Bois was during the McCarthy era. Within the African-American tradition, perhaps only the government's treatment of Paul Robeson comes to mind as more heinous than that of Du Bois, particularly because Robeson's censorship prevented him from earning a living through concert performances and recording sessions."

Only after a long legal battle did Du Bois win a passport. He was a socialist and then a communist, which meant to the government he was evil. He opposed the use of nuclear weapons, which meant he was un-American.

Du Bois tells a thousand times told tale. But it must be repeated again and again and again.

"Not a single Southern legislature stood ready to admit a Negro, under any conditions, to the polls," Du Bois writes. "Not a single Southern legislature believed free Negro labor was possible without a system of restrictions that took all its freedom away. There was scarcely a white man in the South who did not honestly regard Emancipation as a crime and its practical nullification as a duty."

But despite every reason to be bitter, Du Bois kept his "faith in the ultimate justice of things," that one day "men will judge men by their souls and not their skins." Sadly, that day is far distant.

Sparks Tribune, Aug. 7, 2003

War criminal Kissinger

Political cynics love to say that there isn't a dime's worth of difference between the Democratic and Republican parties. It's true to a great extent. For the past two decades Democratic positions on the issues are barely distinguishable from the Republican mantra of property over people.

But the saying is untrue when it comes to appointments. In the past 20 years the Republicans have made bad appointments to the Supreme Court in Sandra Day O'Connor and Clarence Thomas.

O'Connor, appointed by President Reagan in 1983, was the first woman named to the court so few senators could oppose her. Thomas, appointed by President Bush I in 1991, could not be defeated because to vote against a black would be seen as racist. Today O'Connor, a conservative, and Thomas, a reactionary, have solidified the GOP's partisan grip on the court.

Now President Bush II has appointed four key figures in the Iran-Contra scandal, including John Poindexter and Elliott Abrams. Poindexter, convicted of felony for lying to Congress, is heading the Orwell spy office in the Pentagon. Abrams, who admitted withholding information from Congress, is director of Middle Eastern affairs.

All of which leads to the terrible appointment of Henry Kissinger to head the commission investigating 9/11.

Outwardly, Kissinger's credentials are impeccable: secretary of state, national security adviser and foreign policy guru of all gurus. But the terrible truth about Kissinger: he is a war criminal, a mass murderer. He should be tried as the Nazis were at Nuremberg or Milosevic is today at The Hague.

Kissinger has scorned the Constitution, international law and world bodies.

His secret bombing of Cambodia is a crime against

humanity, inflicting death, terror and misery. He engineered a coup in Chile to overthrow the democratic government of Allende. He gave the ok to Indonesia's Suharto to slaughter 50,000 Timorese.

Dr. K sabotaged Vietnam peace talks in Paris in 1968 for political advantage. Then *five* years later he accepted peace terms he could have had in Paris. He long blocked peace efforts in the Middle East.

He authorized wiretaps on his own aides. He pressured President Carter into allowing the deposed Shah of Iran into the United States with disastrous results: seizure of hostages and the U.S. embassy in Teheran. He tried to destroy Daniel Ellsberg, calling him "the most dangerous man in America," for revealing in the Pentagon papers embarrassing facts about U.S. involvement in Vietnam.

Another truth: the man who appointed him, Bush II, does not want to hear the truth about the whys behind 9/11. So Kissinger is a perfect foil. He is incapable of reaching the so-essential whys behind 9/11 because he himself is one of the reasons.

Whitewashing investigations is hardly unprecedented with presidential commissions. See the Warren Commission on the Kennedy assassination, See the Tower Commission on the Iran-Contra link.

Nor is there anything unprecedented about ignoring commission recommendations. See presidential panel findings that marijuana should be legalized or that so-called obscenity should be decriminalized.

The horrible U.S. record in world affairs over the past century is something few Americans know about and even fewer want to hear about. For as Christopher Hitchens writes:

"The United States believes that it alone pursues and indicts war criminals and 'international terrorists.' Nothing in its political or journalistic culture allows for the thought that it might be harboring and sheltering such a senior one (Kissinger)."

Kissinger is a man indifferent to human suffering. He is an accomplished liar: to the American people and to Congress. He is deceitful, manipulative. His penchant for secrecy is exceeded only by the Bush II administration. His three-volume memoirs are misleading, untruthful—and fictional.

He is also ethically challenged. His company, the consulting firm Kissinger Associates, is riddled with global corporation clients to whom he peddles his influence. Hitchens writes again: Kissinger profits greatly "as a private man from the crimes he committed as a public one."

Despite his squalid record, Kissinger is fawned over by the media while he cultivates journalists for his own evil ends. Thus, the media are complicit in his crimes.

Kissinger is Dr. Strangelove personified. He won the Nobel Peace Prize in 1973 for making and prolonging war. It is impossible to satirize such absurdity.

Sparks Tribune, Dec. 22, 2002

The Media

Media undercut 1st Amendment

Journalists love to extol the First Amendment—and it may be the most wonderful 45 words ever put together. But they ignore the fact that self-censorship is rampant in the American media.

The essays in "Into the Buzzsaw" confirm the subtitle of the book: "Leading Journalists Expose the Myth of a Free Press." Edited by Kristina Borjesson, the book deals with stories that were not printed or woefully buried. They indict CBS, Fox and CNN for their coverups, censorship and cowardice. But the blame is spread more widely.

The essence of the damning indictment: the press is free to cover ephemera like White House sex scandals, the death of Princess Diana and the O.J. Simpson trial.

But it is another matter when stories are about CIA involvement in drug trafficking, the October Surprise, U.S. destruction of Iraqi water supplies, U.S. funding of human rights abuses and the TWA 800 crash. Highly sensitive stories like these take more guts than the media have.

Gary Webb was let go by the San Jose Mercury after he exposed the link among the CIA, the Contras and drug-dealing in the Los Angeles ghetto. Worse: the Mercury retracted the story.

Still worse: Webb was dumped on by the Establishment newspapers like the New York Times and the Washington Post. Still "worser": you can bet the farm that the Times, which reviews about 10 insignificant novels each Sunday, won't review "Buzzsaw" because of its explosive "J'accuse."

Borjesson explains the title: "The buzzsaw is what can rip through you when you try to investigate or expose anything this country's large institutions—be they corporate or government—want to keep under wraps. The system fights back with official lies, disinformation and stonewalling."

She should know. CBS would not air her segment saying that the TWA 800 explosion in 1996 was caused by an errant Navy missile. The Pentagon lied about it. The CIA lied about it. The FBI denied the story. But, ah, you see, the Pentagon, the FBI and the CIA were *official* sources. Crash eyewitnesses were not.

The sainted Dan Rather knocked down the story, acting like a government spokesman rather than the journalist he purports to be. The New York Times, relying on lying government sources, debunked the story. The media rule is: the only acceptable sources are official sources.

The reliance on government sources means the country has an Orwellian ministry of truth. The "buzzsaw" crushes the spirit of good and gutsy reporters.

Moreover, as Borjesson and Webb found out, such investigative reporting on nefarious government actions can destroy journalism careers. Ms. Borjesson was fired by CBS, in effect, for daring to rile the Pentagon.

Jane Akre tells how the Fox network sanitized, distorted and slanted a news story about Monsanto chemical. She and her husband were fired by their TV station for refusing to broadcast a story they knew to be false.

Greg Palast tells how the Murdoch news operation has bred "a flock of docile sheep, snoozy editors and reporters who are content to...reprint a diet of press releases and canned stories provided by officials and corporate public relations operations."

CBS refused to air a Palast story of how 50,000 felons, most of them Democrats, were illegally removed from the Florida voter rolls in the 2000 presidential election. Why? "Because it didn't hold up." Who said? Why, Republican Gov. Jeb Bush's office.

Helen Malmgren writes that she is suspicious of any story that comes from corporate public relations companies specializing in "crisis management"—firms that tout cigarettes as healthy and greenhouse emissions good for the Earth.

The CIA, an agency alien to a democracy, controls the media. As Webb writes:

"National news organizations have a long, disappointing history of playing footsie with the CIA, printing unsubstantiated agency leaks, giving agents journalistic cover and downplaying or attacking stories and ideas damaging to the agency."

Aside from upsetting Establishment "truths," investigative reporting, the noblest tradition in journalism, is moribund. It is too expensive, too time-consuming, draws too many libel suits, faces too many pressures to kill stories and runs into too many ruinous conflicts with corporate ownership.

These truths should be taught in journalism schools. But, alas, they won't be. Journalism schools are adjuncts of Establishment media.

Sparks Tribune, Sept. 25, 2002

3 depressing books

Three books have crossed my desk recently, all quite depressing. Why read depressing books? Because the truth, as bitter as it may be, is always better than lies.

As Simone de Beauvoir wrote of the Marquis de Sade in her essay, "Must We Burn Sade?": "He has staked everything on the truth."

The three books are: "9/11" by Noam Chomsky"; "Perpetual War for Perpetual Peace" by Gore Vidal; and "Media Unlimited" by Todd Gitlin.

Chomsky's point: the United States is a leading terrorist state. Vidal's point: this nation that sees itself as perfect is badly, badly flawed. Gitlin's point: image and photo ops, not substance, are everything in politics while society is overwhelmed by a torrent of images and sounds.

A major problem of the American media is that it is far too Establishment-oriented. Its self-censorship is blatant yet unknown to most Americans. The leftist view is rarely presented in any of the Mainstream media.

Vidal's article on the whys behind 9/11 was rejected by The Nation, supposedly a left-liberal magazine. His article explaining Timothy McVeigh, Oklahoma City bomber, was turned down by Vanity Fair.

While the unpopular views of Vidal and Chomsky are available on the Web, cyberspace lacks the impact of a newspaper article, a book or TV broadcast.

Nevertheless, these dissidents have their fans. One reader on the Amazon Web site sized up Chomsky perfectly: "Chomsky is a truth-seeker in a world full of lies. His arguments cut through all the rubbish and nonsense we're all exposed to here in the United States every day."

Chomsky, while decrying the "horrifying atrocities" of 9/11, writes: "We can think of the United States as an innocent victim only if we adopt the convenient path of ignoring the record of its actions."

Among those actions: support for "harsh authoritarian states," "propping up oppressive regimes," overthrowing democratic governments, support for Israel's oppression of the Palestinians, crimes of the CIA and defiance of rulings by the World Court and the U.N. General Assembly.

Vidal, adding to the Chomsky indictment, lists America's numerous wars between Pearl Harbor and 9/11. He leaves out the numerous unjust U.S. wars and invasions in the previous 100 years.

"Once we meditate on the unremitting violence of the United States against the rest of the world, while relying on pretexts that, for sheer flimsiness, might have even given Hitler pause...one begins to understand why Osama bin Laden struck us," Vidal says.

So too with McVeigh who "was enraged by our government's reckless assaults on other societies." He quoted the Justice Brandeis dissent in Olmstead: "Our government is the potent, omnipresent teacher. For good or ill, it teaches the whole people by its example."

The U.S. example for centuries has not just been bad but grossly hypocritical. Its talk of freedom, democracy and a free press is mere rhetoric.

Gitlin rightly complains of the supersaturation of the media: TV, cellphones, CDs, Walkmens, VCRs, the Internet. No wonder no one has time to think about how frightful the Bush administration is.

Meanwhile, everything is an advertising outlet from schools to sports arenas and stadiums, from backs of airplane seats to space over urinals. Logos are plastered all over athletes' uniforms and the clothing of citizens. Phone solicitation is as rampant as it is obnoxious. Video games outgross movies.

Political soundbites on TV have shrunk from 42 seconds in 1968 to 8 seconds today. Candidates get just 11 percent of news time while blathering journalists get 75 percent. Blather and entertainment make money, substance does not.

Making money is all that matters in this sad age of non-thinking, consuming society. Triviality reigns supreme. America is an intellectual disgrace. Democracy is reduced to a sideshow.

Meanwhile, vital people needs like national health and prescription drugs for the elderly go unaddressed. The values of society are all wrong.

The media are hopeless. They do a fine job on 9/11 reporting. But that is easy journalism. What America really needs is investigative journalism. But it is rarely done because it is too costly, too time-consuming and, above all, too offensive to advertisers.

Back to Chomsky. Asked by an interviewer about "Western civilization," he replied with a remark from Gandhi: that Western civilization might be a good *idea*. The United States also might be a good idea if it ever practices what it lectures the world about.

Sparks Tribune, Nov. 14, 2002

Cloying obituaries

One of the most amusing things in the morning paper is the family-composed obituaries. Oh, not that death is a laughing matter. Far from it. But listen, dear reader, to some "for instances."

Many of these obits refer to so-and-so as having "passed away." Not really laughable. It's just that some people are incapable of saying it plainly. Since death has such finality to it, people often cannot bring themselves to say "died." Instead, they use a euphemism, a milder term for harsh reality.

Many such euphemisms have been spawned by the funeral industry, the world's greatest dealer in euphemism. Jessica Mitford ridiculed funeral home euphemisms four decades ago in her classic, "The American Way of Death."

Many of the flowery flights of fancy in the family-composed obits in the Reno Gazette-Journal are hilarious.

The "deceased," a euphemism for the dead, is "returning to her true home." Another: "the Lord reached out his hands and took James home to be with him." Still another waxed poetic:

"God looked around his Garden / and found an empty place. / He then looked down upon his / Earth and saw your loving face… / It broke our hearts to lose you, / But you did not go alone. / For part of us went with you / on the day God called you home."

Other phrases that cause mirth—or at least quizzical eyebrows: "an angel flew off with him," "she went to join her beloved Fred," "Jesus reached down and took him," she "went to sleep in her Lord's love," she "passed on to eternal life," he "went home to be with his Lord," she "will be painfully missed until we are rejoined in heaven," he "passed gently from this earth to fly with the angels" and she "entered the Lord's gates of heaven."

Then their was the sentimentalist who wrote: "While

Mother Nature placed her winter blanket on the Earth, our Lord took Sally's hand and led her into Heaven to be reunited with her parents."

Obviously the fevered believe such cloying purple prose. They exemplify the H.L. Mencken insight that no one ever went broke underestimating the intelligence of the American people.

Obscene picture

An obscene photo appeared on page one of the New York Times recently. It showed Charlton Heston, president of the National Rifle Association, in a three-column picture in color at the bottom of the page.

Heston was holding a flintlock over his head, his mouth wide open in defiance and exultation. He seemed to be challenging his critics to pry the rifle from his "cold dead hands."

Meanwhile, the main story reported that a bus driver had become the 10th sniper victim in the three-week sniper terror near Washington, D.C.

Terrible news judgment

Morris Berman, photographer who died last year, took one of the most famous photos in the history of sports. It showed a bloodied Y.A. Tittle, his helmet off, kneeling in despair in the end zone. Tittle, the New York Giants quarterback, had just been sacked.

In one of the worst news judgments in the history of newspapering, the Pittsburgh Post-Gazette, Berman's paper, did not run the picture. Sports editor's explanation: it had no action in it.

Contest judges had better sense. The picture won the National Headliner award for the best sports photo of 1964. A huge blowup of the photo hangs in the Pro Football Hall of Fame in Canton, Ohio.

Moral of the story: editors are sometimes the most dim-bulbed people in the newspaper business. Look at the outrages perpetrated against Marilyn Newton, Nevada Hall of Fame photographer for the Reno Gazette-Journal. Her art gallery photos are often reduced to near invisibility.

Ode to First Amendment

This columnist often complains bitterly about what's wrong with America policies domestically and internationally. But today let us praise one of America's greatest attributes: the First Amendment.

In France author Michel Houellebecq was prosecuted for saying in an interview that Islam was "the most stupid religion." He was charged with inciting racial hatred. And Italian journalist Oriana Fallaci was tried in Paris for inciting racial hatred by writing in her book, "The Rage and the Pride," that "Muslims multiply like rats."

Fortunately, Houellebecq was acquitted and the case against Fallaci was thrown out because of an error in the legal paperwork. But in America they would have been spared the insult and anguish because of the First Amendment's guarantee of freedom of speech.

However, Jean-Marie Le Pen, leader of the French right-wing, was not so fortunate. He has been fined for saying that the Holocaust was a footnote in history. He was terribly wrong—but has the right to be wrong.

What too few Americans appreciate is that the First Amendment protects opprobium—and stupid opinion.

Sparks Tribune, Jan. 16, 2003

Station 'wins' muzzle award

Jack Newfield, Village Voice columnist, said the greatest gift a newspaper writer can have is freedom. Not more pay, not better benefits. Freedom.

Absolute freedom to write the truth as the writer sees it, absolute freedom to write that the emperor has no clothes on, absolute freedom to call a spade a spade. Sadly, all too few journalists in America have ever had absolute freedom.

Happily, the notable and noble exception is the Sparks Tribune. My Trib column constantly attacks U.S. domestic and foreign policy. It is socialistic and atheistic. Yet I have never been censored by Trib editors since I began the column in 1988.

Other newspapers I wrote for censored me. The Detroit News sometimes refused to run my columns because "they were too radical." It also refused to run my book reviews because they were contrary to the paper's editorial policy. The Columbus (Ohio) Dispatch would not print a nightclub review because it offended a key advertiser.

The Las Vegas Sun would not print some of my columns when the editor called them "treasonous." The Reno Gazette-Journal printed my column in the early 1980s but refused to run one that attacked a sacred cow on the Board of Regents.

So in the main, I am freer in the academy than I was in the newspaper business. Universities have had a great tradition of academic freedom, of free speech—even of speech that offends. Indeed, that is the only reason I support tenure. Without it, too many outspoken professors, or professors with the "wrong" politics, might be fired.

As a fiery individual passionate about politics and public affairs, I cherish the freedom to write and speak without being muzzled.

For about a year I had been broadcasting weekly

commentaries for KUNR, the public broadcasting station at the University of Nevada, Reno. I irked many listeners. One woman who called the station said she loved public broadcast but angrily snapped off the radio "everytime Jake Highton came on."

Brian Bahouth, KUNR news director, valiantly stood behind me despite the considerable heat he had to deflect. He loved to have my commentary aired. He reveled in the controversy. He liked the fact that listeners were exposed to a viewpoint seldom presented by Establishment media.

I admired his courage (never in abundance in the mainstream media).

Then, six weeks ago he censored me. Then he fired me without calling to say way. I had written a column—published by the Trib—harshly critical of UNR President John Lilley in the Mackay mines affair.

I wrote that Lilley was autocratic, squelched dissent, was not the choice of the faculty committee, pushed bad ideas, thought UNR was a junior college before he arrived, was lightly credentialed for a university president, and had plunged into reorganization immediately in order to make his mark before getting "the lay of the land." I also wrote that Provost John Frederick was Lilley's hatchman and sycophant.

I recorded a slimmer version of the column for broadcast on my regular 7:30 a.m. Monday time slot. It was not aired.

Bahouth explained that he wanted balance. Fine. (Except he never demanded balance about my frequent broadsides against President Bush and his band of crude know-nothings.) So then he told me he would probably air my comments during the hour when Provost Frederick appeared on a call-in show. (*That* program also could have used some balance since the articulate Frederick easily swatted away the softball questions—while Bahouth fawned.)

219

My criticism of Lilley was never broadcast. So Lilley gets off scot free—he is almost universally disliked by faculty and staff—and Bahouth proved to be gutless after all.

The censorship reminded me of what we used to call in the newspaper business the Law of Afghanistan. (This was long before Afghanistan got into the news regularly with Soviet and U.S invasions.) The law was that you could blast hell out of the Afghans, halfway around the world who nobody cared about anyway, but you muzzled criticism of people at home.

The Bahouth censorship is profoundly disturbing. It's not that the "Great I" lusted for air time. But the broadcasts were provocative, outside the mainstream. Listeners talked about them, thought about them and discussed them. For that reason I think my silencing is a loss to the community.

Be that as it may, Bahouth deserves a Muzzle Award given to censors by the Jefferson Center for the Protection of Free Speech.

Sparks Tribune, April 24, 2003